S0-BCQ-680

12421623

The
SIGNIFICANCE
of the
WOMEN'S MOVEMENT
to
MARKETING

Landmark Dissertations in Women's Studies Series
Annette Baxter, *Editor*

The
SIGNIFICANCE
of the
WOMEN'S MOVEMENT
to
MARKETING

A Life Style Analysis

Alladi Venkatesh

Landmark Dissertations *in* Women's Studies Series
Annette K. Baxter, *Editor*

PRAEGER SPECIAL STUDIES • PRAEGER SCIENTIFIC

New York • Philadelphia • Eastbourne, UK
Toronto • Hong Kong • Tokyo • Sydney

Library of Congress Cataloging-in-Publication Data

Venkatesh, Alladi.
 The significance of the women's movement to marketing.

 (Landmark dissertations in women's studies series)
 Bibliography: p.
 1. Women consumers—New York (State)—Syracuse.
2. Market surveys—New York (State)—Syracuse.
3. Feminism—United States. 4. Stereotypes (Psychology)
I. Title. II. Series.
HF5415.3.V46 1985   658.8'348   85-19106
ISBN 0-03-069588-0 (alk. paper)

Published in 1985 by Praeger Publishers
CBS Educational and Professional Publishing
a Division of CBS Inc.
521 Fifth Avenue, New York, NY 10175 USA

© 1977 by Alladi Venkatesh

© 1985 by Praeger Publishers

All rights reserved

56789 052 987654321

Composition for this book was provided by the author.
Printed in the United States of America
on acid-free paper

RIDER COLLEGE LIBRARY

Praeger Publishers was privileged to work with Dr. Annette K. Baxter on the creation and development of the Landmark Dissertations in Women's Studies Series. The first books benefited from her careful editing and from the intellectual standards she imposed on all her work. It is our intention to maintain these standards in subsequent volumes despite Dr. Baxter's untimely death.

ACKNOWLEDGEMENTS

This research would not have been possible without the encouragement and support I received from the members of my committee and the cooperation of several others. The chairman of committee Professor George Fisk not only aroused my initial interest in the topic but provided some basic research directions for the study. Professor David Wilemon was a source of inspiration and helped me organize the study by closely following my progress at each stage. Professor Clint Tankersley's assistance in the research design and implementation stage was invaluable. Many constructive suggestions in Sampling Design came from Professor John Chai and Professor Sherman Chottiner who made some insightful comments on the overall research as outsiders to the Marketing area. My association with Professor Louise Solomon, who exposed me to the feminist literature and its various dimensions was very rewarding. To all these individuals, I am deeply indebted.

I also acknowledge my appreciation to the American Marketing Association for awarding me a research grant of $500.00.

My thanks go to Dean L. Richard Oliker who as the Director of Doctoral Programs provided a moral support through my doctoral study.

I extend my thanks to Carolyn Miller and Lorraine Schmidt for their administrative assistance, to Mary VanFossen, Martha Maliwacki and Jo Barriger for the typing assistance.

I am also thankful to Professor Philip Burger of SUNY-Binghamton for his help during the data analysis stage and to Rick Ozer (SUNY-Binghamton) for computer assistance and Dean Murray Polakoff and Dean Charles Gearing both of SUNY-Binghamton for generously allowing me the use of various facilities in the School of Management, SUNY-Binghamton.

Last but not least, my special thanks go to my wife Uma, whose understanding, patience and personal sacrifice make me wonder if this is all worth it.

TABLE OF CONTENTS

LIST OF TABLES

The
SIGNIFICANCE
of the
WOMEN'S MOVEMENT
to
MARKETING

INTRODUCTION

The purpose of this study is to investigate the significance of the women's movement to marketing. For this study the aims of the women's movement are defined as the attempts to bring about a change in the role and status of women in the direction of equality with men. The term feminism embodies these aims. The main focus of this study is on changing life styles of women and their changing roles with implications to marketing.

While popular rhetoric on the women's movement is both enlightening and confusing, in the past decade or so, there has been an increasing emphasis on developing a female ideology separate from and not subservient to male dominance. Much related research has been reported in sociological journals on the changing sex roles and family structure, some of which have formed a basis for this study. The timeliness of this study is further enhanced by the fact that the year this study began (1975) was declared International Women's Year.

Marketing scholars and professionals did not address themselves seriously to the women's movement until very recently. A few studies that have appeared are at best tangential to this subject (Courtney and Lockeretz, 1970; Banos, 1972; Wortzel and Frisbie, 1974). This research project attempts to make a small contribution toward filling this gap by testing hypotheses concerning the attitudes, interests and opinions of three different groups of women toward selective life style dimensions. The approach taken in this study was life style analysis* which has been employed in market segmentation and consumer research studies involving aggregate populations. Multivariate statistical procedures were used to analyze survey data.

In a sense this research is concerned with a current social phenomenon which promises to bring about changes of fundamental importance to marketers,

---

*For an exhaustive review see Wells, 1975.

sociologists, economists and government planners.

OBJECTIVES OF THE STUDY

The general objective of the study is to determine if significant differences exist among three categories of women, labeled as feminists, moderates and traditionalists, across certain life style dimensions.* These three categories are identified on a feminism scale with feminists and traditionalists being the polar groups and the moderates in the middle.

After a review of current literature, and from discussions with members of some women's groups and also based on the researcher's own intuition, it was decided to include three groups in the study. Lipman-Blumen (1972) considered two groups "traditional" and "contemporary" in her research on sex-role ideology. But her subjects were all homogeneous (college graduates in the Boston area) in their general background. Douglas (1976) dichotomized her population into working wives and non-working wives limiting her research to the traditional role. Bailyn (1970), trichotomized her sample wives into traditional, mixed and integrated groups based on how predisposed the respondent was in a career while functioning in the traditional 'housewife' role. Green and Cunningham (1975) use a classification 'Conservatives-Moderates-Liberals' on a continuum described by Arnott's Autonomy Scale (1972). The approach taken in this study is to consider traditionalists and feminists as bipolar categories with moderates as a natural group in the middle. This also implies the transitional character of groupings from one extreme to the other.

The specific objectives of the study are to answer five major questions:

1. Are the life style dimensions common to all the three groups of women selected for the study?

---

*Examples of life style dimensions are innovative behavior, social responsibility, leisure activities, fashion and personal appearance, etc.

2. Do the life style dimensions have the same significance to each group.

3. Do the differences in life style dimensions significantly discriminate between the three groups.

4. Are demographic factors less important in discriminating between the three groups than life style factors.

5. What are the implications of the study to marketers?

WHAT THE WOMEN'S MOVEMENT IS ALL ABOUT*

The history of women's movement between the years 1840-1960 is a relentless struggle to gain social recognition in certain areas such as politics, education, and basic work opportunities (Cnafe, 1972). Most of the concessions extended to women were conceived of as socially reformistic and wherever possible, were incorporated into appropriate laws. The feminist movement of the past decade or so is viewed more as an ideological battle (Rossi, 1969) rather than a mere extension of the previous fight for concessions within the male framework. Popular writers such as Betty Friedan (1963), Germain Greer (1968) and Kate Millet (1970), to mention an important few, have been in the vanguard of this movement calling for fundamental changes in existing family and social systems.

When the movement began, there were two main groups dominating the scene, the so-called "feminists" and the "politicos." The feminists rejected left wing politics and were looking for an ideological revolution "uncontaminated by domination" (Dixon, 1971). The politicos assumed left wing positions and shared the anti-establishment protests of the males in return for the latter's sympathy with their cause. The existing structure of the women's movement seems to have blurred these differences.

Essentially, the women's movement can be considered a revolt against psychological oppression and social and economic discrimination. The movement has

---

*
No attempt is made to present a comprehensive account of the women's movement. Only some basic issues are discussed to provide a background to the study.

been given additional impetus by the success of black movement and, in an effort to establish some kind of spiritual identification with the latter, many feminists regard "male chauvinism" as degrading as "racism." This analogy is seriously questioned by many (Dixon, 1971) who look at the feminist movement as basically an elitist-intellectual-middleclass affair (Freeman, 1972).

The most active women's groups that are carrying on an ideological struggle for women's rights are the National Organization for Women (NOW), Women's Equity Action League (WEAL), and National Women's Political Caucus, founded in 1966, 1968, and 1971, respectively. There are several other less active groups which are small and whose goals are similar to the three groups. Then there are those long established women's organizations such as YWCA, National Federation of Business and Professional Clubs, the League of Women Voters who are more traditional and establishment oriented. These organizations have also modified their programs in active response to the issues raised by the feminists.

The basic difference between the recent movement and the past movements can best be summarized in the words of Alice Rossi (1964), a well known sociologist and feminist:

> It will be the major thesis of this essay that we need to
> reassert the claim to sex equality...By sex equality I mean
> a socially androgynous conception of roles of men and women
> in which they are equal and similar in such spheres as in-
> tellectual, artistic, political and occupational interests,
> complementary only in those spheres dictated by physiological
> differences between the sexes....An androgynous conception
> of sex roles means that each sex will cultivate some of the
> characteristics usually associated with the other in tradi-
> tional sex role definitions....This is one of the points of
> contrast with the feminist goal of earlier day, this defin-
> ition of sex euqality stresses the enlargement of the common
> ground on which men and women base their lives together by
> changing the social definitions of approved characteristics
> and behavior of both sexes.

In summary, the feminist movement has addressed itself to such basic issues as redefinition of the concepts of marriage, motherhood and housewifery, equitable sharing of responsibilities between men and women in all walks of life, and removal of the "false image of women now prevalent in the mass media and in the texts, ceremonies, laws and practices of our major social institutions" (Shaffer, 1973).

SOCIAL AND ECONOMIC ROLES OF WOMEN

Quite often a question arises as to whether women can be treated as a single homogeneous group of individuals. This is because they do not cluster in the same way as some other segments of society do, but in fact, belong to a wide variety of racial, ethnic, economic, religious and national affiliations which might make their treatment as a single group unrealistic.

But as Rossi (1965) points out, to the extent that these affiliations in no way liberate women fully and do not prevent ultimate discrimination, they can only be considered superficial forces pointing to an ineffective diversity. In other words, women will be regarded as a social and economic minority though not numerical minority, as long as they are subjected to social and economic discrimination.

For the purpose of our discussion, we define "role" as a set of expectations, behaviors and attitudes, considered appropriate to a social position (Znaniecki, 1965). The degree of commitment to a role may be affected by the kind of socialization, rates of social change, and contradictions in the prevalent role definitions. Komarovsky (1946) was one of the first to study how "imbalances in privileges and obligations" exist because of cultural contradictions in the roles of women. That is, although the social situations are changing, these have not been recognized adequately by the existing culture. The social rank of women in almost all societies is derived through kinship attachments to men, early in life to a father and later to a husband (Blake, 1974). A consequence of this can be found in the current methods of social class measurement, which have been seriously questioned by Haug (1973). "There seems to be a general practice to measure the social class determinants as pertaining to the male head of the household ignoring his wife's occupation....The use of the male's occupation as a single indicator of a family's social status may have to be re-examined ...(and this) may lead to considerable distortion of the family's socio-economic status." In the traditional role a woman is adjudged on the basis of how good a wife-mother-homemaker she is. The accompanying traditional values associated with this role are concern for others, dependence, gentleness, nuturance and capacity to express feelings (Carden, 1974). The corresponding male values are aggression, individualism, objectivity, achievement orientation, competitiveness.

These social values are closely linked with the economic roles that have separated men and women from historical times. Writing in 1950, Mead observed, "The home shared by a man or men and female partners, into which men bring the food and women prepare it, is the basic common picture all over the world. But this picture can be modified and the modifications prove that the pattern itself is not something deeply biological" (Mead, 1950). This observation does point to economic sex role differences based on division of labor and specialization that have become sharper with industrialization (Bullough, 1973; Benston, 1969). Sex is one of the criteria on which division of labor rests and according to Bernard (1971), "the precise nature of work specifically assigned to men and women is not universally the same...women clean the streets in the Soviet Union, men do it in the United States (spatial and cultural differences) ...women used to mine coal, now men do. Men used to be school masters, later women took over and now men are returning (temporal difference)". Thus the argument points to the belief that economic roles and role changes are in no way related to biological differences.

Another aspect of the economic roles is the "sex-typing" of jobs. In recent years, women have increasingly participated in the labor force, but they are over represented in certain types of jobs such as nurses, typists, secretaries, elementary school teachers, etc. and under represented in occupationally superior jobs. Although statistics show some definite advancements in women's employment (Blitz, 1974; Waldman and McEaddy, 1974), some authors argued that women's participation was remarkably stable over time because none of the advancements could be accounted for by a deliberate policy to improve women's lot but were the result of minor social and economic forces (Gross, 1968). Evidence seems to suggest, however, that fundamental changes have taken place in certain important areas such as education, employment status, recreation and sports, health, and income, as documented by Ferriss in his "Indicators of Trends in the Status of American Women" (1971). (See Appendix 5 for a more current report on the status of American women).

SOCIAL CHANGE AND MARKETING RESPONSE

Marketers are constantly concerned with the changing environment and the need to adapt themselves to such changes. In recent years, the consumerism movement has led to a series of debates and business responses (Aaker and Day, 1974). The threat to ecology and severe raw material shortages have changed the supply environment of marketing, thus requiring a new set of strategies from marketers (Fisk, 1974). The emergence of black movement and the "black cultural influences on consumption" have been exhaustively studied and the research is well documented (Engel, et al., 1973). More recently, the women's movement and its economic and social significance have aroused much serious thinking on the part of social scientists. Changes occur constantly, some changes are anticipated, some are ignored, some others are not foreseen, a few are greeted with skepticism while some changes assume fundamental importance. The impact of women's movement on marketing is not easy to grasp, but Schultz

(1972) has anticipated some results which are listed below:

1. The women's movement is a forerunner of significant changes in the social values and in the social system.

2. The life styles of women will be significantly affected with some bearing on economic behavior of the consumers at large.

3. The traditional household decision making will undergo significant changes.

4. The economics of the household especially in the allocation of women's time in acquiring and processing commodities will change considerably.

5. As a result of anticipated changes in the life styles of women, we can expect changes in life styles of men.

In the following discussion, a brief analysis will be provided for understanding some major issues which may have impact on marketing.

Changing Family Structure

The traditional family structure in the U.S. includes the bread winning and status giving father, the domesticated wife-mother-homemaker with (or without) children, and their respective role structures. Much discussion is taking place on whether the nuclear family as known to Americans will survive. Essentially, the factors that are being discussed relate to changing family patterns and changing saliency of marriage and parenthood (Keller, 1973). Some of them are already occurring without any expectations that the trend will reverse itself. Blood (1972) has adequately discussed how the family structure changes with increasing education, increasing affluence, decreasing religious influence and changing urban environment. Poloma and Garland (1971), in their study comparing traditional and non-traditional families, argue that the existing family system acts as a barrier to women's advancement outside the family. The same opinion is expressed by Simon de Beauvoir (1953) "Desire for feminine destiny -- husband, home and children -- and the enchantment of love are not always easy to reconcile with the will to succeed."

Poloma and Garland's study (1971) was an empirical research into four categories of families, the traditional, neo-traditional, egalitarian and matriarchal. They concluded that in the traditional family, the wife's career is considered a "hobby" and her income is not generally counted as being essential in meeting the family's needs. In the neo-traditional family, income is needed and utilized to maintain the family standard of living and the wife's professional activity assumes a certain level of importance in any decision the family makes. A third category is the egalitarian family, where the couple truely shares both the duties and rights of the "husband-father" and "wife-mother" roles. A last category which is conspicuous by its absence is matriarchy, in which the wife plays a major economic role.

Changing salience of marriage and parenthood occurs because of the breakdown of traditional systems. According to Rossi (1972) in the traditional set-up "neither men nor women are free to openly reject marriage and parenthood." So invariant is the pressure to marry that many unmarried women are forced to keep intact the desirability of marriage as an end in itself, although they may have personal reasons for rejecting marriage. "If the pressure is strong to accept marriage, it is even stronger to accept maternity. Women are not free to say that they do not want children, or after they have them, to indicate they do not enjoy many aspects of child care."

The reason for changing views on marriage can be attributed to the historical transition of marriage from an "institutional" to a "companionship" arrangement. While the institutional approach reflects a normative framework embedded in duty bound tradition and religion, the companionship approach stresses such values as love, companionship and mutual gratification of emotional needs (Mulligan, 1972). A result of this is increasing number of divorces because there is no traditionally dictated obligation to preserve marriage at any "cost."

Other forces acting against the traditional family system include the changing views on abortion, diminishing role of family as transmitter of cultural values, increasing economic independence of women and alternatives to existing form of marriage (Davids, 1971).

Two-Career Family

One development which is becoming more and more commonly recognized among social scientists is the two-career family. In its well developed form it seems to strike at the very heart of "sex-linked division of labor," which places the husband in a demanding occupational role while the wife devotes her time and energy to a basically ancilliary role. In a traditional situation, women, if employed, are in second level jobs and derive their occupational status through their husbands.

However, women entering the labor force now are more educated than their predecessors, and also more women are entering professional and technical jobs which have been traditionally male dominated. Further, more women are thinking seriously of career possibilities that are not secondary to their husbands' and this is what is leading to a "two-career" family system. Although the "two-career" family is an exception rather than the rule, indications are that it will become more common in the future (Holmstrom, 1972).

What are the major consequences of "two-career" family system? It is expected that the roles of both husband and wife will deviate from the much theorized "instrumental" (task oriented) roles of men and "expressive" (socio-emotional) roles of women (Parsons, 1949). The traditional concepts of masculinity and feminity may be altered confirming the adrogyny theory advocated by Rossi (1964). The wife will probably continue to play, for some time, a "super woman" role which combines career, housewifery and motherhood, but eventually will choose her priorities that may have an effect on child bearing and child rearing patterns. The decision regarding the occupational mobility of the family will not be a male decision, nor will be decisions related to usage of time and leisure behavior (Long, 1974; Rapoport and Rapoport, 1969).

The two-career family also creates stresses and strains on women. Dowdall (1974) has observed that the woman who holds a paid full-time job is responding to a "complex combination of social, psychological and economic factors in the environment." In a recent study involving women in twelve countries, Robinson, et. al. (1972) found that employed men have relatively large amounts of leisure time while working women spend their weekends catching up on their housework.

If the two-career family system were to become an acceptable pattern in well developed societies, the changing environment may well have serious implications to marketers. For the present, however, the two-career family is only an exception.

A REVIEW OF RELEVANT RESEARCH INVOLVING WOMEN IN MARKETING AND RELATED AREAS

Traditionally, a marketer's interest in women as consumers has centered around the roles of wife, mother, homemaker, and hostess, or single girl preparatory to the above mentioned roles. A brief review of representative studies are discussed here with implications to marketing.

Whyte (1962) studied women in the role of corporate wives. In this role she was expected to fully participate in the "corporate family" to ensure professional advancement of her husband.

In their classic study, Rainwater, et. al. (1962) made an in-depth analysis of the life styles of blue-collar wives and compared them with their middleclass counterparts. Some of the major conclusions relate to the social and economic goals of the working class women, their daily activities, and their belief and value systems.

In a rather selective study, Eli Ginzberg (1965) attempted to analyze the
life styles of educated women. He concluded that they were individualistic,
socially influential, politically minded and supportive. He also found that
many women believed that family obligations, in a traditional sense, should be
honored regardless of the public status of the woman. Rossi (1966) criticized
this study for its methodological flaws.

Joesting (1971) reports a comparative study of members of women's liberation movement and non-members. She found that the members displayed significantly
higher means on creativity, originality and risk-taking measures than the non-
members. In terms of family background and other demographic variables, no
significant differences were found. The study covered a sample of twenty-five
subjects in each group and it is very difficult to accept its external validity.

Searls (1966) was concerned with the "leisure role emphasis of college
graduate homemakers." She found a high correlation between the age of homemaker
and community welfare activity. As for two other areas of leisure, "self-
enrichment" and "recreation," age did not reveal significant differences. In
like manner, she was able to establish certain relationships between socio-economic characteristics and types of leisure activities.

Lopata's study (1971) was about women who perform the social role of housewife and live in an urbanized region of the United States. Her sample included
suburban housewives, non-working housewives and working housewives living in the
greater Chicago area. A major finding of this study was that a majority of women
considered the roles of mother, wife and housewife in descending order of importance. Roles outside the family (career women, volunteer worker, etc.) which
may be called "social roles" were given least importance. The data was collected
in the late fifties and may not represent current thinking.

Lipman-Blumen (1972) made a comparative study on traditional and contemporary
women. These two types were described to be the bi-polar categories on a contin-

uum based on sex-role ideology, i.e., belief systems, values about appropriate behavior of women. She found significant differences in modes of achievement, educational aspirations, and hierarchy of values. No such differences were found in socio-economic indexes.

A variety of articles and research studies has been reported in the past two decades on household decision making (Davis, 1970, 1971; Blood and Wolfe, 1960; Foote, 1961; Sheldon, 1973). In these studies the main emphasis was given to the family power structure governing the behavior of husbands and wives, family life styles and behavior patterns. The concept of family life cycle has also been a well research topic in consumer behavior (Fisk, 1963; Wells and Gubar, 1966). However, the sensitization of marketing to the changing female roles outside the traditional frame of reference is a rather recent effort as can be seen from the following:

> Appeals have been made to advertisers not to stereotype women as sex objects, simple-minded housewives, or cute secretaries (Willet, 1971).

> A major category of changes in the economic situation of women leading to complete equality with men has been predicted (Weiss, 1971).

> Marketers have been asked to take note of shifting female market so that they are not caught off guard (Cadwell, 1971).

> Women have acquired new status symbols -- resulting in a switch from material goods to personal, intellectual and cultural modes of expression (Miles, 1971).

> A recent in-house management letter within the General Electric Company (1972) discusses the business implications of equal rights of women and warns that 'the first and foremost need is to recognize that the women's rights movement and the trend to a greater participation by women in the labor force are indeed long-range trends and not temporary trends.'

In recent years, some articles in marketing journals have examined the role portrayals of women in advertisements. Courtney and Lockeretz (1970) concluded that "feminists are justified in saying that advertisements do not present a full view of the roles women play in American society." Wagner and Banos (1972), in a follow-up study, found some improvement in the role portrayal of women. Wortzel and Frisbie (1974) were concerned with the question of how role portrayals in advertisements affect the desirability of the product. They found no conclusive evidence that one had any effect on the other. An interesting contribution to the marketing literature has come from Douglas (1976) who tried to compare cross-cultural differences between working and non-working wives in the U.S. and France. McCall (1976) recently identified some trends that make it necessary to identify a new category of women "the work-wife" whose life style "is producing a new set of marketing needs and attitudes that will revolutionize products, distribution, institutions and promotion." Green and Cunningham (1975) examined family purchase decisions in the context of feminine role perceptions. Although their research falls largely into the general framework "family purchase decisions" as traditionally known to marketers, it incorporates some demands of changing women's roles.

Life Style Analysis

The concept of "life style" is not new to marketing. A closely related concept "psychographics" was developed in marketing based on the research by Lazarsfeld (1935), Dichter (1958), Opinion Research Corporation of America (1959), and Koponen (1960). Although psychographics and life style research have been used interchangeably or at least with overlapping meanings, the current approach of researchers appears to make a clear distinction between the two. "Psychographics" refers to studies that place comparatively heavy emphasis on generalized personality traits. Analysts who prefer the term "life style," on the other hand, tend to focus their attention on broad cultural trends, leisure activities, use of time for work and entertainment and other similar activity patterns which may include personality traits (King and Tigert, 1971; Wells, 1975).

Life style has been defined in broad terms representing a "distinctive mode of living of a society or segment thereof;" or as "a totality of behavior comprising the characteristic approach to life;" or as "a concept which deals with time and energy allocations" (Lazer, 1963; Andreasan, 1967; Demby, 1974)

Lazer views life style as a systems concept. "It embodies the patterns that develop and emerge from the dynamics of living in a society" (Lazer, 1963). His approach is represented in the model in Figure 1.

Figure 1. Life Style Hierarchy (Lazer, 1963)

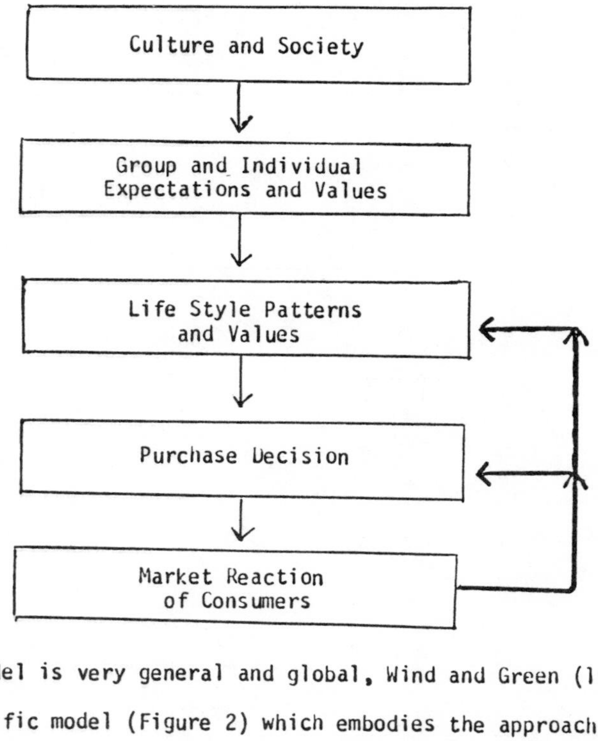

While Lazer's model is very general and global, Wind and Green (1972) present a more situation specific model (Figure 2) which embodies the approach taken by Pessemier, et. al. (1966); Tigert (1969, 1972); Wells (1968); Wells, and Tigert (1971); and Hustad and Pessemier (1974).

In a clear articulation of tnis approach, Hustad and Pessemier (1974) use the term "Activity and Attitude Research" maintaining that:

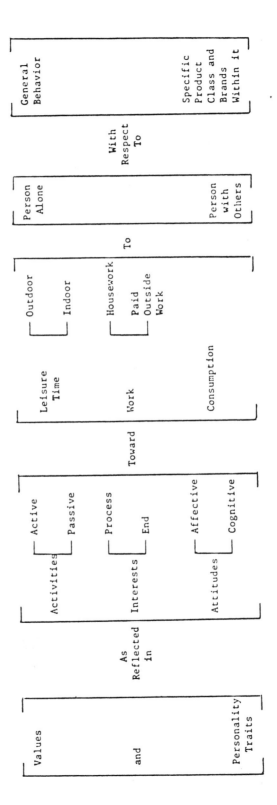

Figure 2. A Classification of Life Style Characteristics (Wind and Green, 1972)

This includes middle range variables and generally de-
emphasizes general personality traits on the one hand
and pure brand preferences or purchase intentions on the
other...Activity and Attitude research is the systematic
development and use of relevant Activity and Attitude
measures to quantitatively describe and predict the purchase and/or consumption of specific products or brands
...When demographic variables, personality variables and
affective measures such as intentions and preferences
are added to what we have narrowly defined as Attitude
and Activity variables, the analyst and manager will
have a complete set of measures.

Pursuant to their approach, Hustad and Pessemier present an interesting and
useful diagram (see Figure 3) "which describes man (or woman) in terms of his
(her) activities (mental and manifest)." It describes a spectrum of social
psychological constructs which include at one extreme more permanent personality
traits resulting in behavior resistant to change, and at the other, object preferences which are subject to rapid change and are formed in specific contexts.
Implied in this model is a life style research orientation which establishes a
trade off between "marketing specificity" and "degree of stability."

Life style research has been used in market segmentation (Frank and Strain,
1972; Pessemier, Burger, Tigert, 1967), for identifying broad consumption patterns
(Wilson, 1966; Tigert, et al, 1971), and in advertising and media research (Ziff,
1974; Young, 1971). As Tigert (1973) points out, it "seeks to quantify activities,
interests, opinions and behavior by systematically researching through a relevant
set of dimensions specific to the problem at hand." A study by New Paper Advertising Bureau (Wells, 1975) is reported to have resulted in eight psychographic
segments of a national sample of males. In a product specific segmentation
study of stomach remedy users, four segments were identified (Pernica, 1974).
In a study on homemaking living patterns, Wilson (1966) identified several life
style dimensions which he considered relevant in studying women in homemaking
roles.

The basic interest of a marketer in studying the life styles of consumer

Figure 3. Relation of Measurable Psychological Characteristics
to Manifest Activities (Actions or Responses)
(Hustad and Pessemier, in Wells, 1974)

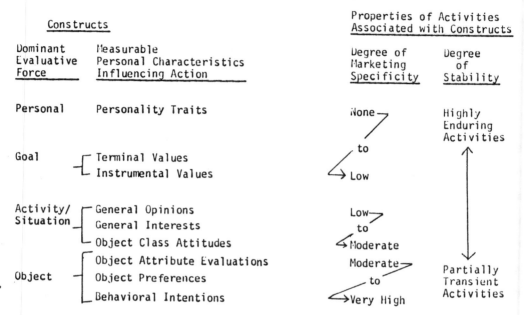

groups lies in discovering new opportunities, developing appropriate marketing

strategies and modifying existing approaches to advertising and market planning.

It is the basic thesis of this study that the women's movement is a significant

social change and merits a serious study. A recent definitive statement issued

on the subject in a report published by Advertising Age (NARB, 1975) highlights

this point. The special report, published in its April 21, 1975 issue, concerns

itself with "advertising portraying or directed to women." The major conclusions

relating to the present role portrayals are similar to those reached in the

Courtney and Lockeretz study (1971). Basically, four stereotypes of images have

emerged in current advertisement. They are as follows:

● A woman's place is in the home

● Women do not make important decisions

● Women are dependent on men and need their protection

- Men regard women primarily as sex objects -- they are
  not interested in women as people.

he report describes in some detail the social and economic trends and changes
n living patterns among various groups of women. It makes some positive
ecommendations for constructive portrayals and positive appeals.

A further justification for undertaking the present study arises from the
ontrast provided by Koponen's findings (1960) and Demby's (1974) comments.
oponen concluded in his study that "men were higher in their expression of
eeds for achievement, autonomy, dominance, sex and aggression. Women received
igher scores on association, assistance, dependence, order compliance and self-
epreciation." Demby (1974) reacts to this by saying "one might warn that as
he role of women changes in society, the latter type of response may change over
ime -- very directly as a result of the effects of the women's liberation move-
ent." Joesting (1971), infact, found that "on the creativity, elaboration,
riginality, and risk taking measures, the women's liberation members had sig-
ificantly higher means than did their peers who were not involved in women's
iberation."

election of Life Style Dimensions

In reviewing the literature and through discussions with well informed
ources, the following major topics have been found to be of concern to women in
eneral and feminists in particular:

- Career commitment (Holmstrom, 1972; Rapporport and Rappoport, 1969)*
- Child care and orientation (Smith and Sternfield, 1972; Berger, 1971)
- Homemaking (Durbin, 1972)
- Problems of employment (Rossi, 1965; Epstein, 1969)

---

* References in parentheses are only representative of the sources where
hese topics are discussed. They are by no means exhaustive.

- Attitude toward marriage (Whitehurst, 1973; Roy and Roy, 1970)

- Contemporary issues (Freeman, 1972)

- Sex equality in all spheres of life (Rossi, 1964)

- Abortion (Spaulding, 1975)

- Occupational and social status (Bernard, 1968; Acker, 1973)

- Sexual sterotyping (Millett, 1969; Van Gelder, 1973)

- Political and civil rights (Chafe, 1972; Steinem, 1972)

In the present study the selected dimensions for analysis include social psycho-logical, personality, behavioral and demographic variables. The study is not product specific but is aimed at understanding a movement that is likely to affect future product consumption patterns which reflect life style changes. The selected dimensions include the following:

- Innovative Behavior

- Social Responsibility

- Opinion Leadership

- Attitude Toward Television

- Self-Confidence

- Frozen Foods

- Life Simplification Products

- Leisure Mindedness

- Magazine Readership

- Role Portrayal of Women in Advertisements

- Fashion and Personal Appearance

- Toys and Sex Symbolism

Some of these measures have already been used by marketing researchers in the past. The general approach to the life style analysis stems from the scenario developed in Tables 1 thru 4 consisting of four dimensions, (a) Family

tructure, (b) Marriage, (c) Career Conmitment and (d) Masculine-Feminine
ctivities. Each of these dimensions is broken down into three categories
or orientations), Traditional, Transitional and Futuristic. The last cate-
ory is deliberately labeled "Futuristic" because it signifies the polar
pposite of "Traditional" orientation. The "Futuristic" trend already exists
n certain segments of the society. The shift from "Traditional" to "Futuristic"
s not sudden but "Transitional" in character. Consequently a middle category
abeled as "Transitional" has been introduced to complete the sequence. The
imensions are not mutually exclusive, but have an interacting influence over
ach other. However, in a conceptual sense they are treated separately.

In Table 1 the scheme proposed analyzes the changing family structure.
oth male and female roles are included to complete the picture. These role
hanges signify some basic structural changes within the context of the family.

Table 1   Family Structure

Traditional	Transitional	Futuristic
read Winning Father	Bread Winning Father and Mother	Bread Winning Father and/or Mother
tatus Giving Father	Status Giving Father	Status Giving Father and/or Mother
omesticated Wife and Homemaker	Liberated Wife and Homemaker	Egalitarian Husband/ wife Homemaking roles
omesticated Mother	Liberated Mother	Egalitarian Father/ Mother Roles

Table 2 has been developed with reference to three factors, meaning of marriage, alternative to marriage as an institution, and the criterion which makes marriage meaningful to the woman.

Table 2   Marriage

Traditional	Transitional	Futuristic
Institutional and Religious Meaning of Marriage	Institutional and Companionship Meaning of Marriage	Companionship Meaning of Marriage
Low Acceptance of Divorce as Alternative	Higher Acceptance of Divorce as Alternative	Modified Nature of Marriage Makes Divorce Trivial
Social and Economic Security for Woman an Important Criterion (Marriage is therefore socially desirable)	Some Security and some Freedom for Women Important Criteria (Marriage is still socially desirable)	Freedom will replace Security as More Women Become Independent (Expediency overrides social desirability)

Table 3 attempts to capture the basic issues under Career Commitment. "The two-person career is quite common and consists of the vicarious participation of wives in the professional role of their husbands who occupy high commitment positions..." (Johnson and Johnson, 1976). At the other extreme is two-career family which affects a relatively small but important contingent of American women..." The basic issues are (a) who has the career, (b) the nature of the career in terms of husband-wife roles and (c) the effect of career on family.

Table 3   Career Commitment

Traditional	Transitional	Futuristic
Only Husband has a Career	Husband has a Career- Wife has a Job	Career of both Husband and Wife are Important
Only Husband's Career affects Location of Family and bringing up of Children	Mainly Husband's Career affects Location of Family and bringing up of Children	Both Careers are In- volved in Location of Family and bringing up of Children
Two-Person Career, i.e. Wife Helps Husband in his Career Advancement	One-Person Career, i.e. Husband does not expect Wife's Contribution to the same extent	Two-Career Family. Each Pursues Her/His Own Career

Table 4 looks at the Feminine-Masculine Activities Dimension. In the traditional roles, feminine activities are basically 'expressive' and are in- tended to maximize the welfare of the families while masculine activities are 'instrumental', directed toward enhancing the male self-esteem or fulfilling the male ambitions. Bailyn (1970) classified categories as related to (a) Career, (b) Family and Home, (c) Leisure and Recreation, (d) Religion, (e) Com- munity Affairs, (f) National and International Betterment. Haavlo-Mannila con- structed a scale of specific social activities from most feminine to most masculine in her study "Sex Differentiation in Role Expectations and Perfor- mance." Bardwick (1971) makes a distinction between feminine patterns of behavior and non-feminine patterns of behavior. While biologically determined activities are unchangeable even in a changing environment, other activities will most likely undergo change especially in their relative emphasis. An illustration of how there changes will occur is given in the following table.

In the traditional environment the high feminine to low feminine activities are well established. In the transitional stage the change takes place within the context of traditional setting. In the futuristic stage a shift occurs resulting in the sharing of activities between men and women within the home and family environment. There is, however, a high emphasis on career and professional pursuits.

Table 4   Feminine-Masculine Activities

Traditional	Transitional	Futuristic
High Feminine Feminine (Unambivalent)	Feminine (Ambivalent)	Feminine (Achievement Oriented)
High Emphasis on Home Centered, Family Oriented Activities	High Emphasis on Home Centered, Family Oriented as well as Social, Cultural, Educational Activities	High Emphasis on Career Professional Activities
Medium Emphasis on Cultural, Social, and Educational Activities	Medium to Low on other Activities	Shared Emphasis on Others with men
Lowest Emphasis Career, Profession and Public Life Activities Low Feminine or High Masculine		

METHODOLOGY

Methodology can be defined as the basic principles and framework of organized investigation within which procedures and techniques are selected and articulated. Procedure is a general form of operating within any investigation. Technique is different from procedure in that it is a "specific fact finding" or "manipulating operation" adapted from the basic procedure (Festinger and Katz, 1953; McKinney, 1957; Kerlinger, 1973). In this study, the basic methodology was empirical and inductive, that is -- generalization of the results based on the examination of a sample of cases within a defined universe. The procedure followed was a survey* which includes (a) sample design, (b) construction of questionnaire, (c) collection of data from participation sample of respondents and (d) analysis of the data using statistical techniques. Multivariate statistical techniques were used to analyze data and examine relevant hypotheses. A flow chart of the "Methodology" section is given in Figure 4. The specific hypotheses to be tested** include the following and are stated in the null form:

H1: Life style dimensions are common to all the three groups.

H2: Hypothesized dimensions and extracted dimensions (factors) will be the same when all the groups are combined.

H3: Life style dimensions do not significantly discriminate between the three groups.

H4: There is no significant difference between the groups on the basis of demographic variables.

---

*An alternative to this is an experimental procedure in which data is gathered by means of direct observation.

** Although the hypotheses are listed as above, it will not be possible to test all of them in a statistical sense. Some of them will be verified by other means.

Figure 4   METHODOLOGY FLOW CHART

Phase No.   Item Explanation   Remarks

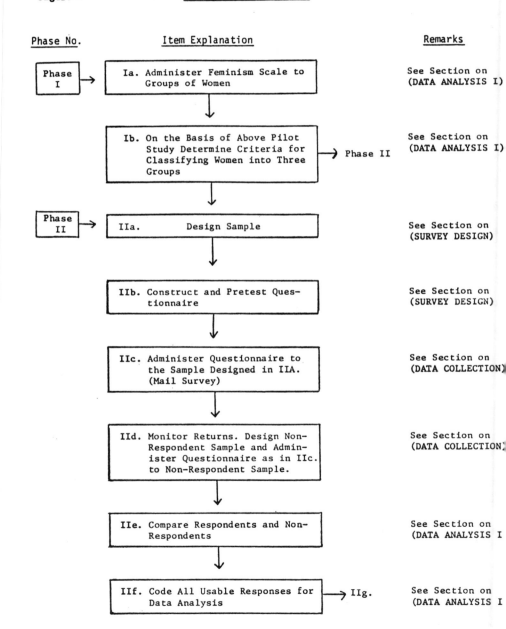

Phase I → Ia. Administer Feminism Scale to Groups of Women — See Section on (DATA ANALYSIS I)

Ib. On the Basis of Above Pilot Study Determine Criteria for Classifying Women into Three Groups → Phase II — See Section on (DATA ANALYSIS I)

Phase II → IIa. Design Sample — See Section on (SURVEY DESIGN)

IIb. Construct and Pretest Questionnaire — See Section on (SURVEY DESIGN)

IIc. Administer Questionnaire to the Sample Designed in IIA. (Mail Survey) — See Section on (DATA COLLECTION)

IId. Monitor Returns. Design Non-Respondent Sample and Administer Questionnaire as in IIc. to Non-Respondent Sample. — See Section on (DATA COLLECTION)

IIe. Compare Respondents and Non-Respondents — See Section on (DATA ANALYSIS I

IIf. Code All Usable Responses for Data Analysis → IIg. — See Section on (DATA ANALYSIS I

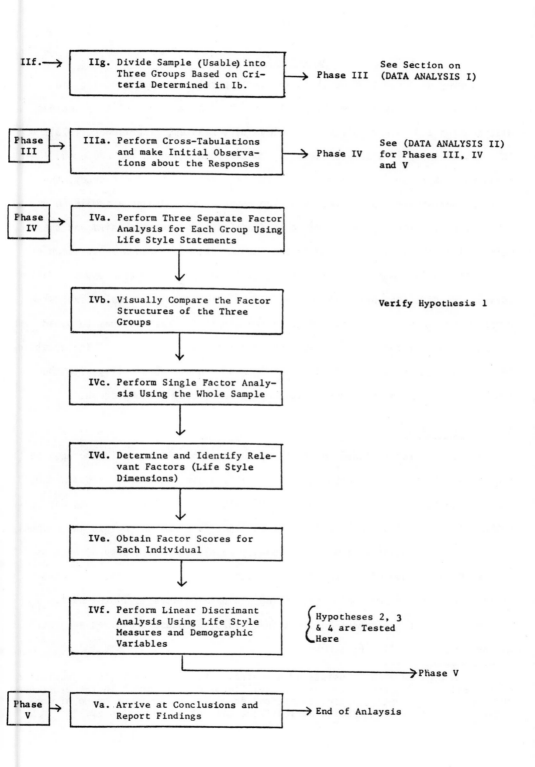

IIf.→ IIg. Divide Sample (Usable) into Three Groups Based on Criteria Determined in Ib. → Phase III   See Section on (DATA ANALYSIS I)

Phase III → IIIa. Perform Cross-Tabulations and make Initial Observations about the Responses → Phase IV   See (DATA ANALYSIS II) for Phases III, IV and V

Phase IV → IVa. Perform Three Separate Factor Analysis for Each Group Using Life Style Statements

IVb. Visually Compare the Factor Structures of the Three Groups   Verify Hypothesis 1

IVc. Perform Single Factor Analysis Using the Whole Sample

IVd. Determine and Identify Relevant Factors (Life Style Dimensions)

IVe. Obtain Factor Scores for Each Individual

IVf. Perform Linear Discrimant Analysis Using Life Style Measures and Demographic Variables   Hypotheses 2, 3 & 4 are Tested Here

→ Phase V

Phase V → Va. Arrive at Conclusions and Report Findings → End of Anlaysis

SURVEY DESIGN

"Survey Research studies large and small populations by selecting and studying samples chosen from the populations to discover the relative incidence, distribution and interrelations of (relevant) variables," (Kerlinger, 1973). The present study is a sample survey of female population in the age group 18-45 residing in Syracuse urbanized area. Given the objectives of the study, the most appropriate method of conducting the research was through a sample survey. The data collection instrument was a self-administered questionnaire and the method of establishing contact with the respondents was through mail. Each of these issues, (a) sampling design, (b) questionnaire construction and (c) mail survey, are discussed below in detail. These three are not mutually exclusive but somewhat interrelated. The size of the sample for instance has to be adjusted because of the generally low response rate in mail surveys. The questionnaire construction is influenced by the lack of contact possibility with the respondent, which requires the questionnaire to be easy to comprehend.

A. SAMPLE DESIGN

The population included in the study consists of all women in the ages between 18-45 living in the urbanized area* of Syracuse, New York, as defined by the U.S. Census Bureau in their report HC(3)-161, 1970. This age group was selected bearing in mind that the feminist movement is of recent origin and comparisons become more meaningful within a younger population. The city of Syracuse was selected because of the convenience to the researcher and equally important, it has been a venue for various marketing and opinion surveys in the past.

According to the census information of 1970, Syracuse urbanized area was divided into the following segments:

---

* An urbanized area "consists of a central city or cities (with a population of at least 50,000) and surrounding closely settled territory." On the other hand an SMSA (Standard Metropolitan Statistical Area) is "a county or group of contiguous counties which contains at least one city of 50,000 or more..."

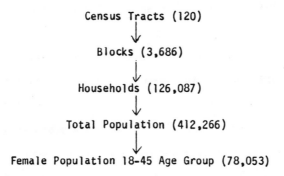

Syracuse Urbanized Area (1970 census)

Census Tracts (120)

Blocks (3,686)

Households (126,087)

Total Population (412,266)

Female Population 18-45 Age Group (78,053)

No figures or approximations were available for more recent years. However, according to the Syracuse City Planning Office, Syracuse population was expected to be rather stable and the projected increase in 1970-76 was less than three per cent over 1970 figure.

Sampling Method

General - The sampling method used was a three-stage stratified cluster sampling to the household level. Cluster sampling is used in surveys for reasons of cost reduction and administrative convenience.

All the 120 census tracts in the Syracuse urbanized area were grouped into 104 primary sampling units (PSU's). Six strata were formed using the 104 PSU's and from each stratum two PSU's were selected on a probability basis. From each PSU, eight blocks were randomly picked making them secondary sampling units (SSU's). In the third stage, households were selected from each block on a random basis and questionnaires were mailed to households without any established procedure for respondent selection procedure. Ideally, one would have liked to implement the scheme suggested by Kish (1949), or Trodahl and Carter (1964) or Bryant (1975). But the costs involved made it impossible to do so.

However, the need to use any respondent selection scheme was obviated by two assumptions. The first assumption made was that very few households would have two females in the age group 18-45 and any bias in violation of this assumption would be negligible. A second assumption was that any household would have either 1 or 0 females in the relevant population. The census figures show that there are 126,087 households compared to the female population (18-45 age group) of 78,053 which is a ratio of 1.61 to 1. The approach taken in this study was to compute the sample size of females and simply multiply the resulting value by a factor of 1.61 which would give the number of households to which the questionnaires would be sent. In a sense, this procedure satisfies the condition under which Kish (1949) sees no need for respondent selection, the condition being "if the respondent is uniquely determined, e.g. head of household or homemaker."

Sampling Frame

"A frame is a means of access to the universe or a sufficient portion there of" (Deming, 1960). According to Deming, care must be taken to avoid four basic mistakes in constructing a frame. They are, (a) missing elements, non-coverage, incomplete frame, (b) clusters of elements in one listing, (c) blanks or foreign elements and (d) duplicate listings. Problems relating to frame construction were minimized by using maps provided by the Census Bureau. These maps were fairly up-to-date to the block level and were cross-checked with the maps prepared by the Syracuse Fire Department in 1975. Since all mailings were sent to households, instead of individual respondents, the most current listing of all household addresses as provided by Polk and Company formed the basis for the study. This listing was published in 1975 and on verification with the City Planning Office, Fire Department and an Advertising Agency, it was found acceptable for survey purposes. The directory is published annually by the company and its 1975 edition was considered fairly up-to-date. A strong recommendation for using the directory comes from the well known sampling expert Seymour Sudman (1976, p. 58). According to him

>"There is no list of all the population or households
>in the United States................................
>At the local level, however, population and household
>lists are available for most medium-sized cities in
>the range of about 50,000 to 800,000 people. About
>1400 of these directories are published by R. L. Polk
>and Company (6400 Monroe Boulevard, Taylor, Michigan
>48180). The directories are usually available for free
>use at the local public library or the chamber of com-
>merce office, as well as for sale by Polk. For sampling
>purposes, most directories contain both an alphabetical
>list of names of residents and business and a street ad-
>dress directory of households. Since the directories are
>revised every 2 or 3 years, the street address directory
>is reasonably accurate. It misses only new construction
>that occurs after the directory is published. The alpha-
>betical list is subject to greater error over time, for
>many families and individuals will move in or out of the
>area or to some new address. Although the directories are
>subject to listing errors, these are usually corrected in
>subsequent directories. Overall, the quality of the lists
>is usually as good or better than the lists that could be
>obtained by a careful researcher who starts from scratch
>with new listers. Of course, the use of existing lists is
>far cheaper."

The sampling method used was a three-stage stratified cluster sampling requiring the following steps:

Formation of the PSU's (Primarily Sampling Units)

The Syracuse urbanized area is comprised of 120 census tracts which are uniquely defined with boundaries clearly mapped for identification. They were conveniently regrouped into 104 PSU's by combining very small tracts with geographically contiguous census tracts wherever possible. Consideration was given to socio-economic differences between the census tracts so combined. Specifically, mean family income, education and non-white population were considered. Census information was available on these items.

Formation of Strata

A total of 6 strata were formed using 104 PSU's. The strata varied in size with respect to the number of PSU's included and the population. Stratification was based on researcher's judgment and the characteristics used were socio-economic. The idea behind stratification is that an increase in precision of the sample estimate can be accomplished by realizing homogeneity within the strata. Although one stratifies the population on the basis of characteristics under study, it was not possible in the present case because no prior knowledge existed about the attitudes of women in various census tracts, regarding feminism and related issues. However, Hansen, et al (1953, Vol. I, pp. 229-230) recommend stratification on the basis of some correlated data which in the present case were certain types of demographic information. Since a study of literature suggests that feminist movement is middle-class-white inspired, stratification was carried out on the basis of three socio-economic characteristics: (a) mean family income
(b) level of education
(c) ratio of white to non-white population

After some judgment and trial and error, it was decided that six strata would be formed. Care was taken to ensure some heterogeneity between strata and homogeneity within strata. Table 5 shows the details of strata formation.

Determination of Sample Size

Although the design involves multi-stage stratified cluster sampling, the problem of determining sample size under simple random sampling (SRS) will be discussed as a basis for eventual determination of the sample size.

Under SRS, when estimate of proportions is under question, sample size is computed as follows:

$$n = \frac{t_\alpha^2 \, PQ}{d^2} \qquad \text{which can be expressed as,}$$

$$n = 100 \, \frac{Q}{P}$$

when $\alpha = .05, t = 2$ (app.) and $d = .2 \, P$ and,

where P is the proportion of the population assumed to have the characteristic under study

Q is $(1 - P)$

α is the specified probability of exceeding the permissible error

t_α is the normal deviate corresponding to the probability α

d is the maximum permissible error

In our present study let us assume that the objective is to estimate the proportion of women who can be classified as feminists in female population between ages 18-45. From the literature (Lipman - Blumen, 1972) we can assume that the proportion of feminists is 0.2. It does not really matter if the actual proportion turns out to be different. Cornfield (1951) has demonstrated that "while the actual precision attained depends to some extent

TABLE 5   FORMATION OF STRATA

Stratum Number	Number of PSU's In Each Stratum (m_h)	Number of Blocks In Each Stratum (SSU's)	Total Population In Each Stratum	Population of Women (18-45) Age Group In Each Stratum	Housing Units In Each Stratum	Mean Family* Income	Education* (High School Graduates Among 25 or Over) (Per Cent)	Non-White* Population (Per Cent)
1	11	301	45,559	9,202	17,347	$ 5,210- 8,788	25-60	10-50
2	6	185	28,364	7,553	7,665	9,748-12,325	45-79	10-31
3	19	517	55,169	10,514	19,957	7,991- 9,716	31-55	0.1-2.6
4	40	1,504	147,357	27,383	45,155	10,206-12,915	45-79	0.0-5.0
5	19	758	92,837	15,464	23,924	13,069-16,653	55-81	0.0-1.7
6	9	421 / 3,686	42,980 / 412,266	12,039 / 78,053	12,039 / 126,087	17,230-27,496	54-87	0.1-0.7

* These values signify the range from the lowest value census tract in the stratum to the highest value.

on the initial value of P assumed, the dependence may be of no practical importance ..... It (the initial estimate) has served its purpose and now disappears from sight." Using a P value of 0.2 we have:

$$n = \frac{4 \times 0.2 \times 0.8}{(0.2) \times (0.2) \times (0.2) \times (0.2)} = 400$$

The rel-variance is given by $\frac{Q}{P} = 4$ and this value will be used later on in determing the sample size under multi-stage cluster sampling.

In computing the ultimate sample size, the methods suggested by Hansen, et al, (1953, Vol. I and Vol. II) were mostly used with modifications. Essentially, the procedure was as follows:

- Computation of the rel-variance of the estimator in cluster sampling (V_{cl}^2)
- Computation of the sample size which would give minimum rel-variance
- Selection of the sample size among possible values based on cost consideration
- Upward adjustment of the sample size obtained in the previous step assuming a certain rate of non-response.

The formula used for computing the rel-variance of the three stage cluster sampling is given by: *

$$V_{cl}^2 = \frac{V^2}{m\,\bar{n}\,\bar{\bar{q}}} \left[\delta_1\,\bar{n}\,\bar{\bar{q}} + 1 + \delta_2\left(\frac{\bar{\bar{}}}{q} - 1\right)\right]$$

V_{cl}^2 is rel-variance of the estimator

V^2 is rel-variance between listing units within the primary strata

m is the number of PSU's included in the sample

$\bar{n}$ is the average number of SSU's selected from the PSU's

$\bar{\bar{q}}$ is the expected value of the average number of listing units to be included in the sample.

---

* Notations explained in Table 6.

Table 6   SAMPLING NOTATIONS

	Sample	Population
Number of Respondents (Third Stage Units) in hij th block	q_{hij}	Q_{hij}
Number of Blocks (Second Stage Units) in the hi th PSU	n_{hi}	N_{hi}
Number of PSU's in the hth stratum	m_h	M_h
Number of Strata	h	h
Feminism Score of the Respondents	x_{hijk}	X_{hijk}
Summations	$q_{hi} = \sum_{j}^{n_{hi}} q_{hij}$	$Q_{hi} = \sum_{j}^{N_{hi}} Q_{hij}$
	$q_h = \sum_{i}^{m_h} q_{hi}$	$Q_h = \sum_{i}^{M_h} Q_{hi}$
	$q = \sum_{h}^{L} q_h$	$Q = \sum_{h}^{L} Q_h$
	$n_h = \sum_{i}^{m_h} n_{hi}$	$N_h = \sum_{i}^{M_h} N_{ni}$
	$n = \sum_{h}^{L} n_h$	$N = \sum_{h}^{L} N_h$
	$m = \sum_{h}^{L} m_h$	$M = \sum_{h}^{L} M_h$

Table 6 (Con't.)

Average Values		
	$\bar{\bar{q}}_{hi} = \dfrac{q_{hi}}{n_{hi}}$	$\bar{\bar{Q}}_{hi} = \dfrac{Q_{hi}}{N_{hi}}$
	$\bar{\bar{q}}_{h} = \dfrac{q_{h}}{n_{h}}$	$\bar{\bar{Q}}_{h} = \dfrac{Q_{h}}{N_{h}}$
	$\bar{\bar{q}} = \dfrac{q}{n}$	$\bar{\bar{Q}} = \dfrac{Q}{N}$
	$\bar{q} = \dfrac{q}{m}$	$\bar{Q} = \dfrac{Q}{M}$
	$\bar{n}_{h} = \dfrac{n_{h}}{m_{h}}$	$\bar{N}_{h} = \dfrac{N_{h}}{M_{h}}$
	$\bar{n} = \dfrac{n}{m}$	$\bar{N} = \dfrac{N}{M}$

Subscripts   k - Individual Respondent

j - Block (SSU)

i - PSU

h - Stratum

δ_1 is the average within strata measure of homogeneity between listing units within primary units.

δ_2 is the average measure of homogeneity listing units within second stage units.

This is the equation suggested by Hansen, et al, (1953, Vol. 1, page 403) for "planning a survey, for speculating on sampling variances and optimum sample design."

Following Hansen, et al (1953, Vol. 1, page 397), the rel-variance of a ratio estimate r in the case of three stage stratified cluster sampling is given by:

$$V_r^2 = \frac{B^2}{m} + \frac{W_b^2}{m \, \bar{n}} + \frac{\bar{\bar{Q}} - \bar{\bar{q}}}{\bar{\bar{Q}}} \frac{W_w^2}{m \, \bar{n} \, \bar{\bar{q}}} \qquad (1)$$

Where $\frac{B^2}{m}$ is the contribution of the first stage sampling to the rel-variance. $\frac{W_b^2}{m \, \bar{n}}$ is the second stage contribution to the rel-variance and $\frac{\bar{\bar{Q}} - \bar{\bar{q}}}{\bar{\bar{Q}}}$ is the third stage contribution to the rel-variance and $\bar{\bar{Q}}$ is the average number of third-stage units per second stage unit in the population. The terms m, $\bar{n}$, and $\bar{\bar{q}}$ have already been explained earlier in this section. The terms B^2, W_b^2, and W_w^2 would require too much elaboration and space, and the reader is referred to the source.

Using (1) Hansen, et al, are able to restate the V_r^2 in terms of measures of homogeneity δ_1 and δ_2. (See Hansen, et al, Vol. II, 1953, pages 222-223). Thus,

$$V_r \doteq \frac{\hat{V}_2^1}{m \, \bar{Q}} [1 + \delta_1 (\bar{Q} - 1)] + \frac{\hat{V}_2^2}{m \, \bar{n} \, \bar{\bar{q}}} [1 + \delta_2 (\bar{\bar{q}} - 1)] \qquad (2)$$

Where
$$\hat{V}_1^2 = B^2 - \frac{W^2}{\bar{Q}}$$

$$\hat{V}_2^2 = W_b^2 + \frac{\bar{\bar{Q}} - 1}{\bar{\bar{Q}}} \, W_w^2$$

$$\delta_1 = \frac{B^2 - \frac{W^2}{\bar{\bar{Q}}}}{\hat{V}_1^2} \qquad \text{and} \qquad \delta_2 = \frac{W_b^2 - \frac{W_w^2}{\bar{\bar{Q}}}}{\hat{V}_2^2}$$

For elaboration of W^2 see (Hansen, et al, 1953, Vol. 1, page 402).

Under certain assumption, (2) further reduces to, as explained by Hansen, et al (1953, Vol. 1, page 402).

$$V_r = \frac{v^2}{m \, \bar{n} \, \bar{\bar{q}}} \left\{ k_1 \, \delta_1 \, \bar{n} \, \bar{\bar{q}} + k_2 \left[1 + \delta_2 (\bar{\bar{q}} - 1) \right] \right\} \qquad (3)$$

Where $\qquad k_1 = \frac{\hat{V}_1^2}{\hat{V}_2} \qquad k_2 = \frac{\hat{V}_2^2}{v^2}$

Since with ratio estimates (according to the authors) k_1 or k_2 will often be near 1, (3) can further be simplified to:

$$V_r^2 = \frac{v^2}{m \, \bar{n} \, \bar{\bar{q}}} \left[\delta_1 \, \bar{n} \, \bar{\bar{q}} + 1 + \delta_2 (\bar{\bar{q}} - 1) \right]$$

This is the formula used in the present study.

In arriving at the values of δ_1 and δ_2 the approach taken by Hansen, et al, (Vol. 1, 1953, pages 302 and 370) was followed. The first assumption is that measures of homogeneity ordinarily will be smaller for large clusters (primary units) than for small clusters (blocks). This means invariably $\delta_2 > \delta_1$. Hansen, et al (page 302) also point out that "a value of 0.10 for δ is the order of magnitude that is often encountered in sampling city blocks for many types of population items." And in page 370, they comment that "in fact, with δ for blocks equal to 0.10, it would not be unusual for the value of δ_1 for counties to be as small as 0.01 or even considerably smaller." Accordingly, it was decided to assign values for δ_1 and δ_2 as 0.01 and 0.10 respectively.

The determination of values for m, $\bar{n}$ and $\bar{\bar{q}}$ proceeded as follows. As is obvious the product of m, $\bar{n}$ and $\bar{\bar{q}}$ gives the required sample size. It was decided to select two PSU's per stratum because only one PSU would be too small to yield representativeness of the sample in light of the fact that there are only 6 strata. Three or more PSU's would mean high cost of sampling.

Having fixed the value of m (= 12) the next step was to try different combinations of $\bar{n}$ and $\bar{\bar{q}}$ for given m and select m, $\bar{n}$ and $\bar{\bar{q}}$ so as to minimize the value of rel-variance. A decision was also made that the overall sample size would be larger than that obtained under SRS which was 400. However, an additional consideration was the cost constraint which necessitated limiting the initial sample size to 500. In effect, various values of $\bar{n}$ and $\bar{\bar{q}}$ were evaluated and the best combination was: m = 12; $\bar{n}$ = 8; $\bar{\bar{q}}$ = 5, which resulted in a rel-variance of 0.015 for a sample size of 480. In the equation cited earlier, V^2 was set equal to 4 being the rel-variance under SRS so that,

$$V_{c1}^2 = \frac{4}{12 \times 8 \times 5} \ [(0.01 \times 8 \times 5) + 1 + 0.1 \ (5-1)] = 0.015$$

For the sake of sampling convenience it was decided to set $n_{hi} = \bar{n}$, i.e. from each PSU the same number of blocks was to be selected. Therefore, given that the number of PSU's and SSU's from each stratum are fixed the only variable quantity will be q_{hij}, i.e. the number of respondents in each block. This requirement ensures that the overall sampling fraction f is preserved across all listing units.

Using Cost Equation to Adjust Sample Size Based on Estimated Response-Rate (Hansen, et al, 1953, Vol. 1, pages 474-5)

Let n_1 be the number of respondents

n_2 be the number of non-respondents

R_1 be the rate of response   (35%)

R_2 be the rate of non-response   (65%)

$n = n_1 + n_2$ is the size of the final sample

$\hat{n}$ is the size of the sample if response was 100% (= 480)

$\frac{1}{k}$ is the fraction of non-respondents visited

$n_2' = (\frac{1}{k}) \, n_2$ the number of non-respondents visited

Assume cost equation:

$$C = C_o \, n + C_1 \, n_1 + C_2 \, n_2'$$

Where   C is the total cost

C_o is the cost per questionnaire mailing = $0.05

C_1 is the cost per questionnaire of processing returned questionnaire = $0.70

C_2 is the cost per questionnaire both of enumerating and of processing questionnaires obtained by interviews of sampled non-respondents = $5.00

Because this is a mail survey, a realistic response rate was set equal to

$$k = \sqrt{\frac{C_2 R_1}{C_o + C_1 \, R_1}} \quad = \quad \sqrt{\frac{5 \times .35}{.05 + (.7)\,(.65)}}$$

$$= \sqrt{\frac{1.75}{.05 + .455}} \quad = \quad \sqrt{\frac{1.75}{.505}} \quad = \quad \sqrt{3.465}$$

$$= 1.86$$

Further $n = \hat{n} \, [1 + (k - 1) \, R_2]$

Substituting values:

$$n = 480 \, [1 + (1.86 - 1) \, (.65)]$$

$$= 480 \, [1 + (.86) \times (.65)]$$

$$= 480 \, [1 + 0.559]$$

$$= 480 \, (1.559) = \underline{748}$$

Sample size required for this survey is 748. However, because questionnaires were being mailed to households, the number of households receiving the questionnaires would be 1,204 (= 748 x 1.6), 1.6 being the ratio of households to females in the population.

Selection PSU's, SSU's and Respondents from Each Stratum

From each stratum two PSU's are selected on the basis of probability proportionate to size (PPS). From each PSU so selected, eight blocks were chosen on the basis of PPS. If P_1 is the probability of selecting a PSU from a stratum and P_2 is the selection probability of a block from each PSU then the number of respondents to be selected from each block should satisfy the equation:

$$f = P_1 \times P_2 \times \frac{\text{respondents from each block}}{\text{total from each block}}$$

'f' which is the sampling fraction is given by $\frac{748}{78053}$ = .0096 where the sample size is 748 and population is 78,053. From the above equation it is easy to solve for the number of respondents to be sampled from each block. Since, in fact, questionnaires were being mailed to households rather than individual respondents, the number of households to be sampled is obtained by multiplying the number of respondents from the above equation by a factor of 1.6.

See Table 7 for the selection of number of households from each stratum according to the method discussed above.

Selection of Households

The identification of blocks and household addresses was done with the help of the directory published by Polk and Company.

TABLE 7. SAMPLE SELECTION

(1) Stratum Identification Number	(2) Total Number of PSU's in the Stratum	(3) Population of Women (18-45) in the Stratum	(4) Identification Number of PSU Selected from the Stratum	(5) Identification Number of Census Tracts Included in the PSU	(6) Population of Women (18-45) in Selected PSU	(7) Probability of Selecting the PSU from the Stratum (6)÷(3)
1	11	9,202	1	25	630	.068
			9	51	1,136	.123
2	6	7,553	32	43	2,687	.36

(8) Total Number of Blocks in the Selected PSU for the Sample	(9) Block Identification Numbers	(10) Population of Women (18-45) in Each Block Included in the Sample	(11) Probability of Selecting the Block from the PSU (10÷6)	(12) Number of Respondents from Each Block	(13) Number of Households from Each Block
18	102	36	.056	6	10
	103	42	.066	7	11
	104	73	.115	12	19
	106	23	.037	4	6
	205	47	.074	8	13
	302	23	.037	4	6
	304	27	.042	4	6
	305	69	.108	4	6
				Total 49	Total 77
32	106	46	.040	8	13
	202	22	.019	4	6
	204	26	.023	4	6
	303	30	.026	5	8
	404	14	.012	2	3
	406	23	.021	4	6
	407	33	.029	5	8
	503	17	.022	3	5
				Total 35	Total 55
40	104	38	.014	3	5
	110	39	.014	3	5
	208	95	.035	6	10
	212	14	.005	1	2
	213	299	.111	20	32
	305	112	.042	8	13
	311	164	.061	11	18
	404	17	.006	1	2
				Total 53	Total 87

TABLE 7. SAMPLE SELECTION (CONT'D.)

(1) Stratum Identification Number	(2) Total Number of PSU's in the Stratum	(3) Population of Women (18-45) in the Stratum	(4) Identification Number of PSU Selected from the Stratum	(5) Identification Number of Census Tracts Included in the PSU	(6) Population of Women (18-45) in Selected PSU	(7) Probability of Selecting the PSU from the Stratum (6) ÷ (3)
			14	45	969	.13
3	19	10,514	22	14	613	.015
			29	26	443	.042

(8) Total Number of Blocks in the Selected PSU for the Sample	(9) Block Identification Numbers	(10) Population of Women (18-45) in Each Block Included in the Sample	(11) Probability of Selecting the Block from the PSU (10÷6)	(12) Number of Respondents from Each Block	(13) Number of Households from Each Block
44	104	21	.022	1	2
	202	42	.044	3	5
	401	13	.014	1	2
	406	27	.028	2	3
	408	76	.078	5	8
	501	34	.036	2	3
	502	30	.031	2	3
	510	42	.044	3	5
				Total 19	Total 31
22	102	37	.060	8	13
	104	36	.059	8	13
	106	32	.052	7	11
	201	63	.102	13	21
	202	59	.096	12	19
	203	51	.083	11	18
	304	16	.025	3	5
	308	10	.016	2	3
				Total 64	Total 103
24	103	23	.053	5	8
	108	18	.040	4	6
	201	19	.041	4	6
	202	20	.044	4	6
	205	10	.022	2	3
	303	20	.044	4	6
	305	20	.045	4	6
	306	25	.056	5	8
				Total 32	Total 49

TABLE 7.   SAMPLE SELECTION (CONT'D.)

(1) Stratum Identification Number	(2) Total Number of PSU's in the Stratum	(3) Population of Women (18-45) in the Stratum	(4) Identification Number of PSU Selected from the Stratum	(5) Identification Number of Census Tracts Included in the PSU	(6) Population of Women (18-45) in Selected PSU	(7) Probability of Selecting the PSU from the Stratum (6)÷(3)
4	40	27,383	36	4	941	.034
			40	19	649	.024
5	19	15,464	84	72	2,501	.162

(8) Total Number of Blocks in the Selected PSU for the Sample	(9) Block Identification Numbers	(10) Population of Women (18-45) in Each Block Included in the Sample	(11) Probability of Selecting the Block from the PSU (10÷8)	(12) Number of Respondents from Each Block	(13) Number of Households from Each Block
44	105	42	.045	25	44
	201	23	.025	14	22
	203	23	.025	14	22
	302	50	.053	30	50
	305	30	.032	18	30
	306	26	.028	16	26
	401	22	.022	13	21
	501	23	.026	13 Total 143	21 Total 232
28	103	40	.062	24	38
	104	31	.048	19	30
	105	25	.038	15	24
	205	21	.033	12	19
	301	26	.041	16	26
	304	27	.042	16	26
	407	19	.029	11	18
	409	15	.022	9 Total 122	14 Total 195
60	101	233	.093	37	59
	109	17	.007	3	5
	113	16	.006	3	5
	116	23	.009	4	6
	207	118	.047	19	30
	215	64	.026	10	16
	307	8	.003	1	2
	311	14	.006	2 Total 79	3 Total 126

TABLE 7. SAMPLE SELECTION (CONT'D.)

(1) Stratum Identification Number	(2) Total Number of PSU's in the Stratum	(3) Population of Women (18-45) in the Stratum	(4) Identification Number of PSU Selected from the Stratum	(5) Identification Number of Census Tracts Included in the PSU	(6) Population of Women (18-45) in Selected PSU	(7) Probability of Selecting the PSU from the Stratum (6)÷(3)
			92	111	1,189	.077
6	9	12,039	97	20	997	.083
			99	71	1,796	.149

(8) Total Number of Blocks in the Selected PSU for the Sample	(9) Block Identification Numbers	(10) Population of Women (18-45) in Each Block Included in the Sample	(11) Probability of Selecting the Block from the PSU (10÷6)	(12) Number of Respondents from Each Block	(13) Number of Households from Each Block
58	201	94	.079	15	24
	205	74	.062	12	19
	211	9	.008	1	2
	305	21	.017	3	5
	313	121	.102	19	30
	317	7	.006	1	2
	320	40	.034	6	10
	906	88	.074	14	22
				Total 71	Total 114
67	112	27	.028	4	6
	206	13	.013	2	3
	308	19	.02	3	5
	311	19	.02	3	5
	402	30	.03	4	6
	404	20	.02	3	5
	409	18	.018	2	3
	510	23	.024	3	5
				Total 24	Total 38
47	101	57	.032	8	13
	104	12	.007	2	3
	111	56	.031	8	13
	115	20	.011	3	5
	210	88	.05	12	19
	303	16	.009	2	3
	307	19	.01	3	5
	901	411	.23	56	90
				Total 94	Total 151

The actual selection process proceeded as follows. Once the blocks were identified for inclusion into the sample, the list of household addresses from each block was obtained from the city directory. The list under each block was serially numbered and the required number of households as determined by the sample allocation was selected on a random basis with the help of a random table. This was repeated for all the blocks in each stratum and thus the total sample was identified.

B. QUESTIONNAIRE DESIGN

In a mail survey, tne researcher's inability to personally contact the respondent makes questionnaire design a crucial part of tne survey. In order to minimize respondent resistance, some measures were taken including (a) elimination of open-ended questions, (b) reduction of the length of the questionnaire, (c) rephrasing of questions after pretesting it and (d) use of rating scales and check lists.

The questionnaire consists of three parts (see Appendix 1). The first part has sixty-three items arranged in a random order and includes tne Feminism scale of Arnott (1972) and 53 items pertaining to certain life style dimensions. All the 63 items are in a statement form and are presented to tne respondent on a five-point scale (strongly agree, agree, neither agree nor disagree, disagree and strongly disagree). The second part is the magazine readership profile and the third part relates to demographic data. Each of the three parts are discussed below in detail.

Feminism Scale - The scale consists of ten items (statements) and nas been developed by Arnott (1972) as Autonomy Inventory Scores. The scale is based on Kirkpatrick's (1936) original scale of items. A similar scale also appears in literature as reported by Dempewolf (1974) consisting of 28 items and tested intensively for its validity and reliability. In tne present study the ten-item scale of Arnott was used for its parsimony and also because it has been used in an earlier marketing study by Green and Cunningham (1975).

Of the ten items in the Feminism scale, half the items support feminist issues and the other five items show negative support. Each item is presented on a five-point continuum (strongly agree, agree, neither agree nor disagree, disagree and strongly disagree). These categories represent respectively values of 5, 4, 3, 2, and 1 on positive items and 1, 2, 3, 4, and 5 on negative items.

hus an individual could score a maximum of 50 points and a minimum of 10 oints on the Feminism scale.

ife-Style Statements - The approach to the construction of life-style ques- ionnaire follows the general description given by Tigert (1973).

"Typically, life-style questionnaires possess the following character- stics:

1. They contain many questions.

2. They are self-administered, with the life-style section consisting of a series of statements to be answered on the Likert scale.

3. The life-style questions are either general, covering the hypothe- sized dimensions, or product specific, with a large number of questions covering three or four product categories.

4. The statements will be mixed so that successive statements do not pertain to the same dimension.

5. There is no specific limit to the number of statements to be used. It depends on the number of dimensions that are being hypothesized, the time requirements for filling in the questionnaire and also the size of the sample.

6. The life-style items are usually designed to profile market seg- ments. ....."

As in the case of Feminism scale, all items under life-style measures ere presented on a five-point scale with a similar scoring procedure. he following life-style dimensions were included in the study:

Innovative Behavior

Opinion Leadership

Self-Confidence

Social Responsibility

Leisure Mindedness

Attitude Toward Television

Role Portrayal of Women in Ads

Fashion and Personal Appearance

Toys and Sex Symbolism

Life Simplification Products

Frozen Foods

The selection of these life-style dimensions was based on three criteria (a) relevance to feminist movement, (b) relevance to marketing, and (c) measurability. The specific life-style items included under each dimension are given in Table 17. The dimensions themselves are discussed below.

1. Innovative Behavior: Included under this factor are two measures: Venturesomeness and Social Integration. These measures were found to account for large variance in determining innovative behavior by Robertson (1967). They were also positively correlated with each other. Brief descriptions of each of the measures are given below.

    Venturesomeness -- This is the degree to which individuals possess a favorable attitude toward trying new ideas and practices. Operationally, it is defined as willingness to take risks in the purchase of new products.

    Social Integration -- This variable may be defined as the degree of an individual's participation and acceptance within the community.

2. Opinion Leadership: Opinion leaders are those individuals from whom others seek advice and information. Two well known Opinion Leadership scales have been developed by Katz and Lazarsfeld (1955) and Rogers and Cartono (1962). They have been widely used in marketing for identifying opinion leaders in fashions, household products, and appliances (Myers and Robertson, 1972; King and Summers, 1970; Summers, 1970; and Marcus and Bauer, 1964). In the present study the opinion leadership questions were

not directed against any particular products or brands and in this respect it followed the approach taken by Wells and Tigert (1971).

3. Self-Confidence: This measure has implications to marketing behavior especially in the context of persuasibility. Research by Shuchman and Perry (1969), Bell (1967a) and Cox and Bauer (1964) has specifically dealt with this problem. The scale is used in the same manner as developed by Day and Hamblin 1964) and is an indicator of how confident the person is in her own judgment or how defensive she is in her posture.

4. Social Responsibility: This scale has been developed by Berkowitz and utterman (1968) and has been used in marketing by Anderson and Cunningham 1972) in their study on socially responsible consumers.

5. Attitude Toward Television: This life style measure has been adapted from Villani and Lehmann (1975) who examined its stability in two separate tudies conducted in 1971 and 1973.

6. Life Simplification Products: Anderson (1971) used a convenience goods ndex and developed five categories of consumers ranging from "high" to "low" epending upon the number of convenience-oriented appliances and accessories vned. In the present study, since our approach was not so product specific, a dification was used. The research interest is the attitude toward owning hese products.

7. Toys and Sex Symbolism: In their quest for ultimate equality, feminists 'gue that a high degree of stereotyping of roles occurs in the symbolism of ys (Pogrebin, 1973). The basic issue involved is the non-sexist approach to e design and packaging of toys.

8. Role Portrayal of Women in Ads: This dimension was included because ' the interest it has created among many researchers in recent years (Courtney d Lockeretz, 1971; Wagner and Banos, 1973, Sexton and Haberman, 1974; NARB,

1975). It is highly relevant to the present study.

9. Leisure Mindedness: This is a dimension which is logical to any life style study. The use of time for work and leisure has been a major sociological theme (de Grazia, 1964, Dumazedier, 1967). For marketers it is an area of major concern for developing new products and services (Fisk, 1963).

10. Fashion and Personal Appearance: In many life style studies involving women, this dimension has appeared as a stable measure (Wells, 1975).

11. Frozen Foods: This was introduced as a product-specific measure.

Magazine Readership Profile: The media habits of the respondents will have considerable implications to marketing communications. Bass, et al (1969) classified magazines into five categories: (a) Cultural Intellectual, (b) Light Reading, (c) Fashion, (d) Homemaker and (e) Movie, Romance and Crime. Thus, 34 magazines representing these various clusters were included in the study. Each respondent was asked to indicate her reading interest on a five-point scale, 'I Never Read It,' 'I Occasionally Read It,' 'I Read About Half the Issues,' 'I Read About Two of Every Three Issues,' and 'I Read Almost Every Issue.'

Demographic Information: A total of eight items were used in the questionnaire relating to demographic information. They are marital status, work status, household status, religion, race, age, education and family income.

Questionnaire Testing

The purpose of this phase of research was to test the questionnaire for appeal, phrasing, content and length. The first version contained 85 life-style statements and took anywhere between 20 to 30 minutes to answer. After some careful editing the total number of statements was reduced to 63 in the final version. Also, the first version of the questionnaire was 8 pages long.

Through a copy reduction process it was possible to reduce the pages to four. The idea was to minimize respondent resistance by making the questionnaire appear short.

The final version of the questionnaire was distributed to fifty women in the age group 18-45, belonging to different social and economic groups. The length of the questionnaire was found to be satisfactory and the time needed to complete it varied from 10 to 20 minutes. Some statements which were found be ambiguous were rephrased and the final version had minimum changes.

C. MAIL SURVEY

The use of mail surveys in gathering data has become a common practice in the past 40 years and has increased in recent years. A very
comprehensive review of mail surveys has been reported by Scott (1961) and
more recently Kanuk and Berenson (1975) have supplemented Scott's study with
more current information. The advantages of mail surveys are lower cost,
lack of interviewer bias and variability, anonymity of the respondents leading
to better quality of information, respondent's ability to check records and
answer in a thoughtful fashion. The major disadvantages are believed to be
very low response rates, response by persons other than addressees, difficulty
in identifying non-respondents, all leading to greater response and non-
response bias (Blumberg, et al 1974; Hansen and Hurwitz, 1946; Pearlin, 1961;
Franzen and Lazarsfeld, 1945; O'Dell, 1962).

In sample survey literature a variety of methods have been suggested to
increase mail response rate. They include the following: preliminary noti-
fication, survey sponsorship, return envelope with paid postage, personalization, both on the cover letter and envelope, assurance of anonymity, money
incentives, attractive paper and printing, method of postage, follow-ups,
and questionnaire length.

As Kanuk and Berenson (1975) report there is no conclusive evidence on
many of the techniques cited above. Their review of approximately 80 mail
surveys yields the following general results.

Common sense seems to indicate that short questionnaires yield better response
rates than long questionnaires, although within a range there is no research evidence to support this view. There is limited evidence to support that survey
sponsorship by 'respected' institutions increases response. Stamped-return
envelope does encourage response because it facilitates questionnaire return.

Airmail letters and special delivery letters are more effective than other forms of postage. No significant advantages exists for first class over third class, stamped mail over metered, commemorative stamps over ordinary postage. Very limited research evidence supports the view that personalization yields significantly better response than non-personalized letters. Titled signatures appear to have an edge over untitled signatures. There seem to be no reported studies on the effects of cover letter formulation upon the response rate. Assurance of anonymity has no significant effect on response rates. A number of studies indicate that a 25¢ incentive sent with the questionnaire is very effective in increasing response rates. Larger sums may create additional response but the cost exceeds the gains in additional information. Follow-ups and reminders very positively increase the responses, but successive contacts bring diminshing returns. In the present study some precautions were taken to ensure maximum possible response. These are discussed in detail in the section on Data Collection.

DATA COLLECTION

The data collection involved the following steps:

    Mailing questionnaires to sample households

    Monitoring of returns and mail follow-up

    Identifying the sample of non-respondent households

    Telephone follow-up of non-respondent sample

A total of 1,204 questionnaires were mailed to sampled households on April 16, 1976. This was done through the bulk mailing facilities of Syracuse University. The cover letter was sent on the official letterhead of the Management Research Center with the titled signature of the director as evidence of legitimate research and sponsorship. The letter paper was strathmore bond which would give a typed letter impression rather than that of a printed paper. Anonymity was promised by specifically mentioning in the cover letter that (a) information provided by the respondents would be held in strict confidence and (b) all information would be used only in aggregate form. All the letters were mailed with a business reply envelope and return postage guaranteed. (See Appendix 1 for a copy of the cover letter).

The rate of incoming mail was recorded as shown on the following page. On April 26, 1976, a follow-up card was sent to all households who had not responded as of that date. Some researchers recommend sending follow-up cards within a few days of initial mailing instead of waiting till 4/5 weeks (Nichols and Meyer, 1966). Thus, a total of 1,067 households were again contacted through a follow-up card. (See Appendix 1 for a copy of the follow-up card). All questionnaires returned until May 21, 1976, were considered responses. There were 327 questionnaires returned during this five-week period making the response rate 44%.*

---

*The response rate is computed on the basis of 725 females selected for the sample and not 1200 households.

LOG SHEET OF RETURNED QUESTIONNAIRES

	April, 1976:								
	20	21	22	23	[a]26	27	28	29	30
Number Received Each Day	31	0	34	21	20	31	3	27	20
Cumulative	31	0	65	86	106	137	140	167	187

a. No University mail was delivered on weekends April 24, 25, May 1, 2, 8, 9, 15 and 16.

	May, 1976:															
	3	4	5	6	7	10	11	12	13	14	17	18	19	20	21
Number Received Each Day	11	13	20	23	22	10	8	5	5	9	6	5	0	3	0
Cumulative	198	211	231	254	276	286	294	299	304	313	319	324	324	327	327

In sampling the non-respondents, the approach taken followed the suggestion of (Deming, p. 68-69, 1960).

> There is an optimum fraction to use in any survey for
> special pressure on the non-responses. The fraction is
> sometimes 1 in 2, sometimes 1 in 3, sometimes 1 in 4
> depending on costs. If the special interviews on the non-
> responses are going to be especially difficult or costly
> compared with the original interviews, the optimum frac-
> tion may be as low as 1 in 5. I have seen the time when
> the special interviews were extremely difficult....I re-
> duced the ratio in this to 1 in 10 with the hope that 1
> in 10 would be better than a complete blackout of the non-
> responses.

Using this practical wisdom and also because of costs, it was decided that a sample of 60 non-respondents would be selected. The number of households to be sampled was 100, the result of multiplying the non-respondent sample size (60) by a factor of 1.61. One-hundred households were selected with the help of a random table. On June 10, 1976, letters (with questionnaires attached) were sent to them with a request to cooperate. (See Appendix 1 for a copy of the cover letter). A monetary incentive of one bi-centennial silver dollar was offered if the respondent returned the completed questionnaire with her name identified. Wherever possible, telephone contacts were made from the day after the ques-tionnaires were mailed. Thirty-three questionnaires were received over a period of 10 days and only 20 of the respondents took advantage of the offer.

A brief summary of the steps taken for improving overall response rate for the entire survey is given below.

1. Follow-up of respondents was done through a reminder card sent within 10 days of the first mailing.

2. Length of questionnaire - questionnaire was pre-tested and reduced in length from its original form. Some statements were altered which might have appeared confusing.

3. Time of mailing - no particular strategy was used because of inconclusive evidence. However, when the initial mailing was done it was not a holiday time, although the non-respon-dent mailing was done in June.

4. Return envelopes were included.

5. Personalization - this could not be accomplished because individual responds were not identified. Letters were mailed only to the households.

6. Assurance of anonymity was guaranteed.

7. Survey sponsorship - this was done through Syracuse University Management Research Center.

8. Follow-up of non-respondents - telephone calls were made wherever possible. The city directory gives all the telephone numbers listed as on the date of its preparation.

9. Response by persons other than qualified respondents - in order to make sure that the questionnaires were completed by members of the target population, a total of 50 calls were made to selected households to check if females between 18-45 responded to the questionnaire. Only 23 contacts could be made and in 18 cases the response indicated that the questionnaire was completed by a female in the age group 18-45. In remaining 5 households, no answer could be obtained.

10. Appearance of the questionnaire - within possible limits this was accomplished. The questionnaire speaks for itself.

11. Interesting topic/title - it is conceivable that the topic was interesting to some and not to others. The title was, however, carefully selected "Changing dimensions in the life styles of women."

12. Premiums - because of cost limitations, only the non-respondent sample was offered a silver dollar. Only a small increase in the response rate was noticed, presumably because (a) the non-respondents are generally less cooperative, (b) the non-respondents were asked to identify their names. In any case, one should not compare the non-respondents with the respondents for establishing the effect of monetary award. A better comparison would be between non-respondents who received the offer and who didn't, or respondents who received the offer and those who didn't.

DATA ANALYSIS I

Feminism Scores for Classifying Women Into Groups of Traditionalists, Moderates and Feminists

In social science research the classification of human populations into groups on the basis of attitudes is both an art and a science. The Feminism scale used in the present study was developed by Arnott (1972) and has since been used in marketing by Green and Cunningham (1975). (In both these studies the classification of respondents into 3 groups -- traditional, moderate and contemporary -- was based on arbitrary cut-off points, thus raising some questions of research validity.) This error has been avoided in the present study.

A feminism score questionnaire consisting of 2 parts was constructed. (See Appendix 2 for a full description of the questionnaire). The first part includes 6 items which carry a maximum score of 25 points and a minimum of 2 points. Of the 6 items, 3 and 6 are self-designating requiring the respondent to describe herself on Liberal-Feminist and Conservative-Traditional dimensions. The second part of the questionnaire is Arnott's Feminism Scale with all the 10 items. Arnott's scale was later included in the life-style questionnaire used for the main survey.

The feminism score questionnaire was distributed to different groups of women in the Syracuse University area. They included women activists in the University, female students in the School of Management, non-working wives of Syracuse faculty and female employees in the University departments. Out of a total of 180 questionnaires distributed, 120 were returned. Fifteen of them were found incomplete and the remaining 105 were considered for analysis.

Step I: In the first step of analysis, part 1 of the feminism score questionnaire was considered. The sum of the 2 scores on items 3 and 6 were correlated with the scores on all the 6 items in this part. The range of scores on these 2 items combined was 2 to 12. For example, if a person described herself

Extremely Feministic (on Traditional-Feminist dimension) and Extremely Liberal (on Conservative-Liberal dimension), she would receive a maximum score of 12 and for the purpose of this research would be considered as a feminist. Thus, a classification was carried out according to the following system on the basis of combined scores received on items 3 and 6.

Score	Group Classified
1-5	Traditional
6-8	Moderate
9-12	Feminist

The reason for running a correlation between the scores on items 3 and 6 on the one hand and all the 6 items on the other was to establish content validity (Nunnally, 1967, p. 80-81). Items 3 and 6 were considered sufficient to classify an individual into 1 of the 3 groups. However, in order to make sure that this was the case, one had to examine whether they represented the same construct* whose domain could be enlarged to include more items. These items were selected with specific reference to behavior relevant to feminism. The result of this procedure is to confirm the use of self-designating items for classification as is done in other research areas of marketing such as measurement of opinion leadership. The product moment correlation between the 2 sets of scores was a high 0.83 which was very significant.**

Step II: The objective of step II was to establish ranges of scores on the feminism scale that would classify a respondent to one of the 3 groups -- traditionalists, moderates and feminists.

As a first step, the scores on items 3 and 6 from step I were correlated with scores on the Feminism scale. The idea was to check whether a person who

---

*A construct concerns a domain of related observables.

**
   To test the product moment correlation the method suggested by Blalock (1972) (with Z-transformation) was used.

designates herself a Feminist/Liberal would also obtain a high score on the Feminism scale and vice versa. The range of possible values on the Feminism scale are a minimum of 10 and a maximum of 50. The product moment correlation between step I scores and Feminism scale scores was found to be 0.58 which was significant at 0.95 level of confidence.

The classification of individuals was carried out in the next step. For the 3 groups identified in step I corresponding mean scores were computed on the Feminism scale. The cut-off point was chosen as a mid-point between the successive mean scores. The mean values for traditionalists, moderates and feminists were 32, 40 and 46 respectively. Thus, the final classification for the sampling survey was based on the following scores.

Feminism Scale Score	Group Classified
36 and below	Traditionalists
37 thru 42	Moderates
43 thru 50	Feminists

Comparison of Respondents and Non-Respondents

Out of a total of 327 responses received from the respondents, 26 were found unusable. All the 32 questionnaires received from the non-respondent sample were complete and usable. Table 8 gives a comparison between the respondents and non-respondents on some demographic factors. To put matters in perspective, population figures are also shown wherever such figures are available. Because the non-respondent sample is rather small, only some broad observations are possible. First, each demographic variable is discussed individually, and this is followed by some general remarks.

Race - The race distribution among respondents (94% white, 6% non-white) compares very well with population figures (95% and 5%) although among non-respondent sample it was (88% and 12%). Since, to begin with, the non-white population is rather small compared to whites, the difference does not mean much.

Age - Age groups distributions among respondents and non-respondents vary rather significantly. No explanation appears possible except that more females in the 18-24 group probably had left Syracuse area in summer when the non-respondent sample was taken and thus constituted a lower percentage. Once again, the age group distribution of respondents compares favorably with the population distribution.

Education - The differences between respondents and non-respondents on this variable are not totally unexpected. It is fairly well known that higher response rate is positively correlated with higher education. No figures are available for the population because census data is incomplete.

Family Income - Among both the respondents and non-respondents lower income groups are under-represented and higher income groups are over-represented. Generally, income is positively correlated with education, and this explains the differential representation among income groups.

While some differences between the respondents and non-respondents were noticeable, because of the small number of non-respondents, it was felt that the differences could be misleading. Besides, the differences appeared to be less consequential from an overall comparison with the population values. It was, therefore, decided to combine respondents and non-respondents in the absence of any valid reason not to do so.

Coding of Responses

All questionnaires were coded to facilitate transfer of data to IBM cards with 80 columns. Each response was reduced to 2 cards and to enable easy access and operations all the data was transferred to the disc space in the IBM computer facility at State University of New York at Binghamton. Much care was exercised in checking that the data stored on the disc was in identical order

TABLE 8 RESPONDENTS AND NON-RESPONDENTS

	Respondents (n=301) Percentage	Non-Respondent Sample (n=32) Percentage	Combined Respondents and Non-Respondents (n=333) Percentage	Population Syracuse Urbanized Area Percentage
Race				
White	94	88	93	95
Non-white	6	12	7	5
Age				
18-24	34	27	33	34
25-34	36	45	38	33
35-45	30	28	29	33
Education				
Up to High School	24	31	25	Not Available*
Some College	29	34	29	
College Graduates	26	22	25	
Post-Graduate	22	13	21	
Family Income				
0-4999	8	12	9	14**
5000-9999	21	21	21	30
10000-14999	27	33	29	32
15000-19999	18	18	18⎫	26
20000 and above	26	6	23⎭	

*Census data gives combined figures for both sexes. Also
the information relates to adults over 25.

**Census data does not break down income groups above 15,000

with the data on the cards. All computations were done using SPSS Version 6 (1975) developed by the University of Chicago with modifications wherever necessary.

Formation of Groups in the Total Sample

The Feminism scale (see earlier section on questionnaire construction) containing 10 items was embedded in the life style statements in a random order. For each respondent the scores on 10 items were summed and the classification of an individual into one of the 3 groups was carried out. The criterion for classification into one group or the other was based on the cut-off points for each group determined earlier. (See first section under Data Analysis). Accordingly, the following numbers emerged.

Group	No. in Each Group	Percentage in Each Group	Feminism Score Range
Traditionalists	111	33.3%	36 and below
Moderates	109	32.7%	37 thru 42
Feminists	113	33.9%	43 thru 50
Total Sample Size	333		

As is evident from the above figures, each group is almost equal in size.

DATA ANALYSIS II

Some Initial Results

Demographic Variables - Tables 9 thru 16 give a summary of the demographic characteristics of the groups. Each variable is discussed indiv- idually with relevant comments on differences and similarities.

Marital Status - (Table 9) In each group most women are in the married category, i.e., over 60% and the second highest category is "never married" over 20% in each case. The census figures for the Syracuse urbanized area for females over 14 are 60% in the married category and 26% in the 'single' category. The differences between the groups appear negligible.

Age - (Table 10) The differences between the three groups appear to stand out clearly. In the feminists group, 74% of the respondents are between ages 18-30, whereas a low 46% of the traditionalists are in this age category and 64% of the moderates belong here. Similarly, 40% of the traditionalists are in the upper two age categories as compared to 26% of moderates and 17% of the feminists. This supports the basic assumption made in the section on Survey Design of this study which necessitated limiting the target population to younger age group. The women's movement being of more recent origin, this result is not too surprising.

Race - (Table 11) Over 90% in each group are whites and the remaining are non-whites. This compares favorably with the population values (95% and 5% respectively). One consequence of this data is that although it represents the population distribution, the over all results of this study cannot be generalized to non-whites. If one were to conduct a study on the attitudes of non-whites, the design should include them on a disproportionate basis. There appear to be no differences between the groups on the basis of race.

Education - (Table 12) The differences between the groups are very obvious.   There are more feminists in the college graduate and post-graduate categories than moderates or traditionalists. The respective values for the groups are 61%, 43% and 34%. Among lower levels of education (High school grad-uates and below), there are more traditionalists than members of other two groups. A possible explanation for this is that younger females are more educated than older females. Since there are more young women among feminists, there are also more educated women in this group.

Family Income - (Table 13) The data do not appear to reveal differ-ences. The distribution in all cases is centered in the three categories $5,000-9,999, $10,000-14,999, $15,000-19,999, with a total of 22%, 29% and 18% of the entire sample respectively in these categories. The population figures reveal the median family income for the Syracuse urbanized area to be $10,450.

Work Status - (Table 14) In all the three groups the largest proportion are employed full-time; traditionalists 34%, moderates 48%, feminists 42%. And in the total sample full-time employed women constitute 41%, which compares very well with the national average. The major differences between the groups are in the two categories "In School" and "Keeping House." More feminists are still in school, 22%, almost equal to traditionalists (10%) and moderates (13%) put together. There are more traditionalists (34%) "Keeping House" than moderates (16%) and feminists (14%) add up to.

Religion - (Table 15) While there are equal proportions of Protestants in each group (about 36% to 40%), there are more Catholics among traditionalists (50%) as compared to moderates (36%) and feminists (26%). More feminists (16%) classified themselves as belonging to Jewish faith than moderates (41%) and traditionalists (2%).

TABLE 9 MARITAL STATUS

	Married	Widowed	Divorced	Separated	Never Married	Row Total
Traditionalists	75 (67.6)	4 (3.6)	5 (4.5)	4 (3.6)	23 (20.7)	111 (33.3)*
Moderates	68 (62.4)	0 (0.0)	6 (5.5)	7 (6.4)	28 (25.7)	109 (32.7)
Feminists	78 (69.0)	0 (0.0)	5 (4.4)	3 (2.7)	27 (23.9)	113 (33.9)
Column Total	221 (66.4)	4 (1.2)	16 (4.8)	14 (4.2)	78 (23.4)	333 (100.0)

* Figures in Parentheses are percentages.

TABLE 10 AGE

	18-24	25-30	31-34	35-39	40-45	Row Total
Traditionalists	32 (28.8)	20 (18.0)	15 (13.5)	23 (20.7)	21 (18.9)	111 (33.3)
Moderates	42 (38.5)	28 (25.7)	11 (10.1)	11 (10.1)	17 (15.6)	109 (32.7)
Feminists	39 (34.5)	45 (39.8)	10 (8.8)	9 (8.0)	10 (8.8)	113 (33.9)
Column Total	113 (33.9)	93 (27.9)	36 (10.8)	43 (12.9)	48 (14.4)	333 (100.0)

TABLE 11 RACE

	White	Black	Spanish	Asian	Other	Row Total
Traditionalists	102 (91.9)	5 (4.5)	0 (0.0)	2 (1.8)	2 (1.8)	111 (33.3)
Moderates	102 (93.6)	4 (3.7)	0 (0.0)	0 (0.0)	3 (2.8)	109 (32.7)
Feminists	106 (93.8)	3 (2.7)	2 (1.8)	0 (0.0)	2 (1.8)	113 (33.9)
Column Total	310 (93.1)	12 (3.6)	2 (0.6)	2 (0.6)	7 (2.1)	333 (100.0)

TABLE 12 EDUCATIONAL STATUS

	Elementary	Some High School	High School Graduate	Some College	College Graduate	Post Graduate	Row Total
Traditionalists	1 (0.9)	3 (2.7)	.38 (34.2)	31 (27.9)	26 (23.4)	12 (10.8)	111 (33.3)
Moderates	0 (0.0)	6 (5.5)	25 (22.9)	31 (28.4)	28 (25.7)	19 (17.4)	109 (32.7)
Feminists	0 (0.0)	0 (0.0)	9 (8.0)	35 (31.0)	30 (26.5)	39 (34.5)	113 (33.9)
Column Total	1 (0.3)	9 (2.7)	72 (21.6)	97 (29.1)	84 (25.2)	70 (21.0)	333 (100.0)

TABLE 13 FAMILY INCOME

	0-4999	5000-9999	10000-19999	15000-19000	20000-24999	25000-29000	30000-49000	50000 and above	Row Total
Traditionalists	11 (9.9)	18 (16.2)	35 (31.5)	19 (17.1)	11 (9.9)	7 (6.3)	6 (5.4)	3 (2.7)	110 (33.3)
Moderates	8 (7.3)	22 (20.2)	32 (29.4)	25 (22.9)	8 (7.3)	7 (6.4)	6 (5.5)	1 (0.9)	109 (32.7)
Feminists	10 (8.8)	34 (30.1)	28 (24.8)	16 (14.2)	7 (6.2)	8 (7.1)	9 (8.0)	1 (0.9)	113 (33.9)
Column Total	29 (8.7)	74 (22.2)	95 (28.5)	60 (18.0)	26 (7.8)	22 (6.6)	21 (6.3)	5 (1.5)	332 (100.0)

TABLE 14 WORK STATUS

	Full-time	Retired	In School	Part-time	Temp Out of Work	Keeping House	Unemployed	Other	Row Total
Traditionalists	38 (34.2)	4 (3.6)	10 (9.0)	15 (13.5)	0 (0.0)	38 (34.2)	3 (2.7)	3 (2.7)	111 (33.3)
Moderates	52 (47.7)	1 (0.9)	13 (11.9)	16 (14.7)	2 (1.8)	17 (15.6)	7 (6.4)	1 (0.9)	109 (32.7)
Feminists	47 (41.6)	1 (0.9)	22 (19.5)	20 (17.7)	0 (0.0)	16 (14.2)	4 (3.5)	3 (2.7)	113 (33.9)
Column Total	137 (41.1)	6 (1.8)	45 (13.5)	51 (15.3)	2 (0.6)	71 (21.3)	14 (4.2)	7 (2.1)	333 (100.0)

TABLE 15   RELIGIOUS GROUPING

	Protestant	Roman Catholic	Jewish	Other	Row Total
Traditionalists	44 (39.6)	55 (49.5)	2 (1.8)	10 (9.0)	111 (33.3)
Moderates	41 (37.6)	37 (33.9)	4 (3.7)	27 (24.8)	109 (32.7)
Feminists	41 (36.3)	29 (25.7)	18 (15.9)	25 (22.1)	113 (33.9)
Column Total	126 (37.8)	121 (36.3)	24 (7.2)	62 (18.6)	333 (100.0)

Household Status - (Table 16) More traditionalists called themselves housewives (25%) than moderates (15%) and feminists (7%). A large number of feminists (74%) designated themselves as co-heads of household compared to moderates (56%) and traditionalists (46%). However, roughly equal proportion in each group were included in the category of "Head of Household", 18% in the case of feminists.

To summarize, one gets the impression that feminists are younger, with higher educational attainment and enjoy greater sense of independence in terms of work status and household status. The opposite holds true for traditionalists with moderates in the middle. At the same time, no significant differences exist between the groups in marital status, racial mixture and family income.

Life Style Variables (Statements)

The life style variables used in the questionnaire are grouped under various hypothesized dimensions as shown in Table 17. The analysis was carried out for each statement using contingency tables. Each statement had five possible responses, "Strongly Agree," "Agree," "Neither Agree nor Disagree," "Disagree" and "Strongly Disagree." The frequencies under each response were tabulated and a chi-square test performed. Table 17 gives the proportion of respondents in each group who tend to agree with a given statement. Those who tend to agree include the respondents who indicated that either they "Agree" or "Strongly Agree." Out of a total of 63 statements, 27 statements were found not significant. Statements found significant are clustered around two dimensions "Women's Role in Advertising," "Toys and Sex Symbolism," topics which have aroused much discussion among feminists. Statements which are non-significant relate to "Opinion Leadership" and "Frozen Food Consumption." Other dimensions contain statements which are both significant and non-significant.

TABLE 16 HOUSEHOLD STATUS

	Head of Household	Housewife	Dependent	Cohead	Row Total
Traditionalists	20 (18.0)	28 (25.2)	12 (10.8)	51 (45.9)	111 (33.3)
Moderates	20 (18.3)	16 (14.7)	12 (11.0)	61 (56.0)	109 (32.7)
Feminists	18 (15.9	8 (7.1)	3 (2.7)	84 (74.3)	113 (33.9)
Column Total	58 (17.4)	52 (15.6)	27 (8.1)	196 (58.9)	333 (100.0)

TABLE 17   FREQUENCY ANALYSIS OF LIFE STYLE STATEMENTS INCLUDED
UNDER EACH HYPOTHESIZED DIMENSION

(With Chi-Square Test Results)

Variable Number	Life Style Dimension	Variable Mnemonic	Number and Percent of Respondents in Each Group Who Tend to Agree with the Statement[b]			Level of Significance or Non-Significance of Chi-Square Test[d]
			Traditionalists	Moderates	Feminists	
11[a]	Innovative Behavior I often try new ideas before my friends do.	Inn 1	54 (49)[c]	52 (48)	67 (59)	0.0253
21	When I see a new brand of product on the shelf, I often buy it just to see what it is like.	Inn 2	35 (32)	26 (24)	32 (28)	NS
22	I feel I am a member of more organizations than most women are.	Inn 3	22 (20)	15 (14)	20 (18)	NS
32	Sometimes I buy things impulsively and do not feel sorry about it later.	Inn 4	49 (44)	57 (52)	59 (52)	NS
33	I feel I can talk to most people in the neighborhood any time I feel like it.	Inn 5	53 (48)	50 (46)	46 (41)	NS
60	I like people who take risks in life without fear of what may happen	Inn 6	38 (34)	48 (44)	58 (51)	0.0800

a. Variable Number assigned for Data Analysis.

b. Tend to agree included only those who indicated 'Agree' or 'Strongly Agree' in their responses.

c. Figure in parenthesis is percent rounded off.

d. Chi-Square test done using contingency tables with frequency values in cells corresponding to all five categories of responses, 'Strongly Disagree', 'Disagree', 'Neither Agree nor Disagree', 'Agree', 'Strongly Agree'.

TABLE 17 (Con't.)

Variable Number	Life Style Dimension	Variable Mnemonic	Number and Percent of Respondents in Each Group Who Tend to Agree with the Statement			Level of Significance or Non-Significance of Chi-Square Test
			Traditionalists	Moderates	Feminists	
	Opinion Leadership					
14	My friends or neighbors often come to me for advice.	Op L 1	63 (57)	60 (55)	65 (58)	NS
25	I sometimes influence what my friends say.	Op L 2	37 (33)	45 (41)	56 (50)	NS
56	People come to me more often than I go to them for information about brands.	Op L 3	26 (23)	27 (25)	20 (18)	NS
	Self-Confidence					
15	I feel capable of handling myself in most social situations.	S Con 1	87 (78)	82 (75)	97 (86)	0.08
26	I seldom fear my actions will cause others to have a low opinion of me.	S Con 2	48 (43)	61 (56)	44 (39)	0.01
38	It doesn't bother me to have to enter a room where other people have gathered already and are talking.	S Con 3	73 (66)	69 (63)	77 (68)	NS
39	In group discussions, I usually feel my opinions are inferior.	S Con 4	25 (23)	14 (13)	16 (14)	0.0009
46	I don't make favorable first impressions on people.	S Con 5	19 (17)	20 (18)	11 (10)	NS
47	I would feel extremely uncomfortable if I accidentally went to a formal party in ordinary clothes.	S Con 6	61 (55)	48 (44)	58 (51)	NS

Variable Number	Life Style Dimension	Variable Mnemonic	Number and Percent of Respondents in Each Group Who Tend to Agree with the Statement			Level of Significance or Non-Significance of Chi-Square Test
			Traditionalists	Moderates	Feminists	
50	When confronted by a group of strangers, my first reaction is one of shyness and inferiority.	S Con 7	27 (24)	26 (24)	26 (23)	NS
52	I don't spend much time worrying about what people think of me.	S Con 8	61 (55)	60 (55)	62 (55)	NS
55	I am rarely at a loss for words when I am introduced to someone.	S Con 9	47 (42)	54 (50)	64 (57)	NS
	Social Responsibility					
18	It is no use worrying about current events or public affairs; I can't do anything about them anyway.	S Res 1	29 (26)	19 (17)	18 (16)	0.0018
29	Every person should give some of their time for the good of the country.	S Res 2	69 (62)	63 (58)	59 (52)	NS
42	Our country would be better off if we didn't have so many elections and people didn't have to vote so often.	S Res 3	10 (9)	4 (4)	8 (7)	0.0400
43	At school I volunteered for special projects.	S Res 4	64 (58)	67 (62)	79 (70)	NS
	Fashion and Personal Appearance					
19	An important part of my life and activities is dressing smartly.	Fash 1	41 (39)	42 (38)	43 (38)	0.0600

TABLE 17 (Con't.)

Variable Number	Life Style Dimension	Variable Mnemonic	Number and Percent of Respondents in Each Group Who Tend to Agree with the Statement			Level of Significance or Non-Significance of Chi-Square Test
			Traditionalists	Moderates	Feminists	
30	I love to shop for clothes.	Fash 2	55 (49)	50 (46)	53 (47)	0.0010
44	I like to feel attractive.	Fash 3	95 (86)	100 (92)	102 (90)	0.0400
51	I would like to go to beauty parlor as often as I can.	Fash 4	19 (17)	13 (12)	6 (5)	0.0007
58	I enjoy looking through fashion magazines to see what is new in fashions.	Fash 5	67 (60)	69 (63)	64 (57)	NS
63	I like to do lot of partying.	Fash 6	29 (26)	43 (39)	43 (38)	NS
	Television Viewing					
16	Television has added a great deal of enjoyment to my life.	Tel 1	42 (38)	29 (27)	28 (26)	NS
27	I don't like watching television and so I rarely do.	Tel 2	27 (24)	40 (37)	44 (39)	0.0100
40	I watch television to be entertained.	Tel 3	55 (50)	51 (47)	59 (52)	0.0023
45	I watch television more than I should.	Tel 4	32 (29)	20 (18)	42 (37)	0.0180
53	I don't pay much attention to television commercials.	Tel 5	66 (59)	78 (72)	80 (71)	0.0018

Variable Number	Life Style Dimension	Variable Mnemonic	Number and Percent of Respondents in Each Group Who Tend to Agree with the Statement			Level of Significance or Non-Significance of Chi-Square Test
			Traditionalists	Moderates	Feminists	
	Leisure Mindedness					
12	Leisure activities express one's talents better than does a person's job.	Leis 1	54 (48)	45 (41)	38 (38)	NS
23	Leisure activities are more satisfying than a job.	Leis 2	36 (32)	33 (30)	32 (28)	NS
34	Ambitions are more realized on the job than in one's free time.	Leis 3	37 (33)	42 (39)	34 (30)	NS
36	I indulge in sports activities in my free time.	Leis 4	59 (53)	57 (52)	70 (62)	0.0800
37	It is encouraging to see women participate in outdoor sports as men do.	Leis 5	87 (78)	100 (92)	108 (96)	0.0001
48	During leisure time I like to relax by reading a book or listening to music.	Leis 6	80 (72)	89 (82)	106 (94)	0.0200
61	If I am not working, I feel bored.	Leis 7	52 (52)	47 (43)	56 (50)	NS
	Frozen Food Consumption					
13	I couldn't get along without frozen foods.	Fr F 1	20 (18)	20 (18)	22 (20)	NS
59	I depend on frozen food for at least one meal a day.	Fr F 2	28 (17)	13 (12)	12 (11)	NS

TABLE 17 (Con't.)

Variable Number	Life Style Dimension	Variable Mnemonic	Number and Percent of Respondents in Each Group Who Tend to Agree with the Statement			Level of Significance or Non-Significance of Chi-Square Test
			Traditionalists	Moderates	Feminists	
	Women's Role in Advertising					
17	American advertisements picture a woman's place to be in the home.	Ad 1	42 (38)	70 (64)	101 (89)	0.0000
28	American advertisements seem to have recognised the changes in women's roles.	Ad 2	53 (48)	36 (33)	25 (22)	0.0000
41	American advertisements depict women as sexual objects.	Ad 3	49 (44)	61 (56)	92 (81)	0.0000
54	American advertisements depict women as independent without needing the protection of men.	Ad 4	16 (14)	9 (8)	4 (4)	0.0000
	Toys and Sex Symbolism					
20	I would like to see more and more young girls play with mechanical toys.	Toys 1	20 (18)	46 (42)	85 (75)	0.0000
31	I would like to see boys playing with dolls just the way girls do.	Toys 2	12 (10)	33 (30)	74 (66)	0.0000
57	Boys and girls should play with the same kind of toys.	Toys 3	34 (30)	70 (64)	90 (80)	0.0000
	Life Simplification					
24	I consider it essential for most American families to own an automatic coffee maker.	Life 1	13 (12)	1 (1)	5 (4)	0.0010

Variable Number	Life Style Dimension	Variable Mnemonic	Number and Percent of Respondents in Each Group Who Tend to Agree with the Statement			Level of Significance or Non-Significance of Chi-Square Test
			Traditionalists	Moderates	Feminists	
35	I consider it essential for most American families to own a dishwasher.	Life 2	19 (17)	7 (6)	12 (11)	NS
49	I consider it essential for most American families to own a food disposal unit.	Life 3	14 (13)	4 (4)	4 (4)	0.0260
62	I consider it essential for most American families to own a washer and dryer.	Life 4	74 (68)	58 (53)	54 (47)	0.0400

In interpreting the statements, the last column in Table 17 may appear somewhat misleading. The level of significance or non-significance of the chi-square does not appear to truly reflect the differences or similarities that are captured in the previous three columns. The chi-square test was performed on the basis of five exclusive categories of response, whereas in the table the two categories "Agree" and "Strongly Agree" are collapsed into one. For example, the variable number 30 under "Fashion and Personal Appearance" indicates that it is highly significant. But the frequencies are so close to each other (55, 50, 53) that the significant results appears counter-intuitive.

Factor Analysis of Life Style Variables

Factor Analysis* is a powerful numerical technique used for data reduction and for studying interrelationships between large number of variables as bodies of data. It may be used for any of the following reasons:

(a) to identify the factors which can explain the intercorrelations among the variables which have been measured earlier,

(b) to test a hypothesis about the number and nature of factors,

(c) to verify previous findings about the factors using a new sample and,

(d) as a first step in the investigation into the variables which may provide some directions for the future.

The first three objectives constitute the scope of the present study.

An issue in Factor Analysis is the ratio of number of observations to the number of variables involved. This is similar to the degrees of freedom problem in multiple regression. As Rummell (1970, p. 220) points out, "when the interest is only in describing data variability, then a factor analysis will yield such a description regardless of variables exceeding cases in number. When the interest is inference from sample results to universal factors, however, the

---

*See Appendix 3 for technical discussion.

umber of cases should exceed variables....What rule of thumb in determining
he minimum allowable ratio of cases to variables for inference is still a
atter of research taste. Cattell (1952) suggests a 4-to-1 rule of thumb, i.e.,
0 cases for 10 variables."

In the present study, the ratio of number of cases to variables is 2:1
hen separate Factor Analyses are performed on individual group data. Here
he objective is limited to examining the stability of factor structure across
he three groups. In analysis that follows, however, the three groups are
ombined to yield a ratio of 6:1 between the cases and variables.

In the interpretation of factors, two basic criteria are followed. Only
hose factors with a minimum contribution to variance (i.e., eigenvalue) of 1
nd have a conceptual meaning are considered for further discussion. The
inimum contribution to variance is known as Kaiser's rule, which is designed
o "exclude factors not accounting for at least the total variance* of one
ariable" (Rummell, 1970, p. 363). Secondly, the meaningfulness of each factor
s very important, and this is not a numerical or statistical problem but a
ubjective evaluation of the researcher. For example, between two admissible
actors (based on Variance-one criterion), although one of them may have greater
ariance, it may be ignored if it has no theoretical significance, and a factor
ith lower variance selected if it lends itself to greater interpretability
the basis variables clustered under the factor.

A final issue is the determination of number of variables which ought to
considered for each factor. This is based on rotated factor loadings** (the

---

Since all the variables enter the analysis after being reduced to zero
mean and unit variance, the total variance of a single variable is equal
to one.

See Technical Appendix 3 for an explanation of factor rotation.

loading describes the correlation between a factor and a variable) of at least 0.30. Sheth and Tigert (1970) recommend a minimum value of 0.2 while Bass, et al (1969) suggest 0.30. There is no universal opinion on this, but in applied research a loading of 0.30 is more commonly used.

Factor Analysis of Individual Groups

Separate Factor Analyses were performed on each group using all the 53 life style statements. Because the ratio of observations to variables for each group is 2:1, best results were not expected. Table 18 gives the factors extracted in individual group analysis. Also given in the table are each factor's contribution to total variance, and a listing of variables with loadings of at least 0.30 against each factor in descending order of the loadings. Of the 11 hypothesized life style dimensions only one dimension, Social Responsibility, was not extracted. A listing of all life style dimensions with corresponding factor identification number under each analysis is presented in the table.

According to Hypothesis I originally stated, life style dimensions will be common to all groups. This can be verified by visual inspection of Table 18 and is confirmed as holding true from the results presented. The method of visually inspecting factor structures is suggested by Harman (1967, p. 209) as one of various methods. The purpose here is to establish stability of factor patterns across different samples. For a researcher it represents a degree of confidence that he might have in the representation of the same life style structure by "Congruent" factors. The formation of factors, however, is not perfectly congruent. Firstly, the contribution of variance of matched factors* is not the same. Also, the order of appearance of each factor is different in each group

---

*
An example of matched factors (from Table 19) is Factor 1 of Traditionalists, Factor 2 of Moderates, Factor 2 of Feminists, all of which refer to same life style dimension, Self-Confidence. Matched factors are the same as congruent factors.

TABLE 18
FACTOR ANALYSIS LIFE STYLE VARIABLES
BY INDIVIDUAL GROUPS

TRADITIONALISTS

Factor Number and Contribution to Variance	Variable Mnemonic	Factor Loading
1 (4.45)	S Con 7	0.763
	S Con 1	0.760
	S Con 3	0.516
	S Con 5	0.485
	Inn 5	0.440
	S Res 4	0.375
2 (4.08)	Fash 5	0.773
	Fash 1	0.766
	Fash 2	0.627
	Fash 6	0.485
	Op L 2	0.412
	Leis 5	0.356
	S Con 6	0.335
	Fash 3	0.322
	Leis 4	0.316
3 (3.47)	Life 3	0.832
	Life 2	0.621
	Inn 3	0.436
	Life 1	0.423
	Fash 3	0.352
	S Res 3	0.342
	Tel 5	0.310
4 (2.89)	Tel 1	0.806
	Tel 2	0.764
	Tel 4	0.742
	Tel 3	0.515
	Leis 3	0.303
5 (2.40)	Leis 2	0.810
	Leis 1	0.728
	Leis 6	0.441
	Leis 3	0.332
6 (2.21)	Toys 2	0.789
	Toys 3	0.670
	Leis 5	0.328
	Op L 3	0.322
	Leis 4	0.317
	Toys 1	0.311

TABLE 18 (Con't.)

Factor Number and Contribution to Variance	Variable Mnemonic	Factor Loading
7 (1.97)	S Res 2	0.691
	S Con 4	0.648
	Fash 3	0.574
	Leis 3	0.353
8 (1.89)	Ad 2	0.835
	Ad 1	0.529
	Op L 3	0.340
	S Res 3	0.318
	Op L 2	0.303
9 (1.77)	Inn 5	0.462
	Op L 2	0.405
	Ad 1	0.371
	Leis 7	0.327
10 (1.72)	S Res 1	0.813
	Inn 6	0.454
	Life 2	0.385
	Life 4	0.362
	S Res 3	0.339
11 (1.65)	Inn 1	0.687
	Op L 3	0.563
	Inn 6	0.403
	Op L 1	0.345
	S Res 4	0.311
	Leis 3	0.302
12 (1.42)	Inn 2	0.788
	Tel 5	0.449
	Ad 3	0.398
13 (1.36)	Fr F 2	0.744
	Fr F 1	0.675
	Leis 7	0.599
	Toys 1	0.364
	Life 2	0.340
	Op L 1	0.334
	Ad 1	0.309
14 (1.35)	S Con 2	0.701
	Ad 3	0.555
	S Con 3	0.349
	S Con 4	0.341
15 (1.27)	S Con 9	0.715
	S Con 6	0.643
	S Con 3	0.408
	Leis 6	0.349
	Tel 5	0.349

TABLE 18 (Con't.)

MODERATES

Factor Number and Contribution to Variance	Variable Mnemonic	Factor Loading
1 (4.62)	Fash 3 Fash 1 Fash 2 Fash 5 Toys 1 S Con 6 Toys 2 Toys 3 Fash 3	0.752 0.713 0.672 0.636 0.544 0.400 0.367 0.329 0.309
2 (4.36)	S Con 1 S Con 4 S Con 9 Ad 3 S Con 6 S Con 8 Fash 4	0.554 0.454 0.383 0.383 0.361 0.322 0.304
3 (2.77)	Life 3 Life 2 Life 1 Life 4	0.801 0.777 0.605 0.552
4 (2.67)	Tel 2 Tel 1 Tel 3 Tel 4	0.765 0.752 0.637 0.635
5 (2.40)	Inn 3 S Con 1 Leis 6 S Res 2 S Res 3	0.686 0.483 0.459 0.429 0.377
6 (2.22)	Inn 4 Inn 1 S Con 6 Inn 6	0.825 0.653 0.378 0.314
7 (1.99)	Ad 1 Ad 2 Ad 3 Ad 4	0.835 0.678 0.513 0.303
8 (1.94)	Leis 7 Op L 3 Ad 4 S Con 4 S Con 9	0.721 0.525 0.507 0.475 0.311

TABLE 18 (Con't.)

Factor Number and Contribution to Variance	Variable Mnemonic	Factor Loading
9 (1.75)	Fr F 1	0.847
	Fr F 2	0.733
	Fash 4	0.304
10 (1.70)	Leis 1	0.813
	Leis 2	0.783
	S Res 2	0.311
11 (1.62)	Fash 6	0.740
	Leis 4	0.585
	S Res 3	0.558
12 (1.54)	Tel 5	0.736
	S Con 8	0.674
	S Con 9	0.346
	Tel 4	0.313
	Inn 6	0.307
13 (1.42)	Leis 3	0.751
	Leis 6	0.464
	Ad 4	0.452
14 (1.40)	Leis 5	0.837
	Op L 1	0.447
	Inn 6	0.367
	S Con 4	0.333
	Fash 5	0.329
15 (1.29)	Inn 5	0.787
	Toys 3	0.663
	S Con 2	0.478
	Toys 2	0.449
16 (1.26)	S Con 5	0.748
	Op L 3	0.332
	Op L 1	0.418

FEMINISTS

Factor Number and Contribution to Variance	Variable Mnemonic	Factor Loading
1 (4.74)	Fash 3	0.763
	Fash 5	0.715
	Fash 2	0.708
	Fash 1	0.568
	S Con 6	0.484
	Life 4	0.430
	Fash 4	0.323
2 (4.18)	S Con 7	0.754
	S Con 5	0.740
	S Con 9	0.714

TABLE 18 (Con't.)

Factor Number and Contribution to Variance	Variable Mnemonic	Factor Loading
	S Con 1	0.616
	S Con 3	0.432
	S Con 4	0.373
	S Con 6	0.311
3 (3.09)	Ad 4	0.820
	Ad 1	0.781
	Ad 3	0.725
	Ad 2	0.506
4 (2.94)	Life 3	0.779
	Life 1	0.639
	Life 4	0.480
	Leis 3	0.303
5 (2.48)	Tel 2	0.857
	Tel 1	0.751
	Tel 4	0.669
	Tel 3	0.649
6 (2.23)	Fr F 2	0.843
	Fr F 1	0.829
7 (1.89)	Op L 3	0.756
	Op L 2	0.545
	Inn 3	0.531
	Op L 1	0.384
	Fash 1	0.351
8 (1.83)	Leis 4	0.768
	Inn 1	0.451
9 (1.76)	Leis 7	0.764
	S Con 4	0.356
	Leis 3	0.322
10 (1.66)	Leis 1	0.838
	Leis 2	0.837
11 (1.59)	Inn 6	0.712
	Inn 5	0.523
	Tel 5	0.462
	S Con 4	0.343
12 (1.53)	Leis 6	0.755
	S Res 3	0.536
	Ad 2	0.330
13 (1.41)	S Con 8	0.773
	Inn 1	0.410
	S Res 4	0.378
	S Con 4	0.305

TABLE 18 (Con't.)

Factor Number and Contribution to Variance	Variable Mnemonic	Factor Loading
14 (1.36)	Toys 3 Toys 2 Toys 1 Fash 4 Leis 5	0.776 0.727 0.646 0.444 0.365

TABLE 19

LIFE STYLE FACTORS (DIMENSIONS) WHICH

ARE COMMON TO ALL GROUPS

Life Style Dimension	Factor No. In Each Group		
	Traditionalists	Moderates	Feminists
Self-Confidence	1	2	2
Fashion Mindedness	2	1	1
Life Simplification	3	3	4
Attitude Toward Television Viewing	4	4	5
Leisure Mindedness	5	10	10
Toys and Sex Symbolism	6	15	14
Frozen Foods	13	9	6
Innovative Behavior	11*	6	11
Attitude Toward Role Portrayal of Women in Advertisements	8	7	3
Opinion Leadership	11*	16	7

*This factor appears twice because both sets of variables are loaded   a
single factor.

which actually follows from the variance contributions of matched factors not being the same. Secondly, variables loaded on each matched factor are different. Thirdly, the factor loadings of identical variables on matched factors vary. Finally, the order of variables according to their factor loadings in matched factors is not the same. These differences are not only to be expected, but in a way, desirable to demonstrate that the groups are different in composition.

To summarize, the basic hypothesis of common dimensions appears valid but their structure differs across the groups.

Factor Analysis of Life Style Statements
With All Groups Combined

In this stage of the analysis the objectives are:

(a) to see if life style dimensions emerge as hypothesized
     or at least close to their original hypothesized form,

(b) to check if any new dimensions are formed,

(c) to draw over-all inferences on the dimensions.

Table 20 lists the hypothesized dimensions and the dimensions (factors) extracted from Factor Analysis. Table 21 gives detailed information on each
hypothesized dimension together with a listing of variables selected under
each of the dimensions. In the section on questionnaire construction the
theoretical basis for each dimension was discussed. The Table lists the entracted dimensions in descending order of their contributions to variance
(Eigenvalues). Relevant variables with loadings of 0.30 and above are shown
under each factor.

From Table 20 it seems clear that all the hypothesized dimensions were
extracted with the exception of one, Social Responsibility. Two others,
Women's Role in Advertising, and Toys and Sex Symbolism were factored as one
which is now designated as Sex Stereotyping. Similarly, a single hypothesized
dimension, Leisure Mindedness is now formed into two factors Leisure-Work
Attitudes and Active-Leisure Behavior. Although some other factors were extracted with eigenvalues greater than 1 they were left out of the analysis for
two reasons. Firstly, their contribution, although greater than 1, was very
low (lower than the factors accounted for) and secondly, no conceptual meaning
could be attached to them. For as Thurstone observed (Rummell, 1970, p. 477)
"Incidental Factors are almost certainly present in every study. Hence the
investigator should feel free to leave without interpretation those primary

TABLE 20. FACTOR ANALYSIS OF LIFE STYLE VARIABLES (ALL GROUPS)

Hypothesized Dimensions	Extracted Dimensions (Factor Number in Parenthesis)	Remarks
Women's Role in Advertising Toys and Sex Symbolism	Sex Stereotyping (1)	Two Hypothesized Dimensions formed into one
Self-Confidence	Self-Confidence (2)	
Fashion and Personal Appearance	Fashion and Personal Appearance (3)	
Television Viewing	Television Viewing (4)	
Life Simplification Products	Life Simplification Products (5)	
Leisure Mindedness	Leisure-Work Attitude (6) Active-Leisure Behavior (8)	One Hypothesized Dimension formed into two.
Innovative Behavior	Innovative Behavior (7)	
Opinion Leadership	Opinion Leadership (9)	
Frozen Foods	Convenience Foods (10)	
Social Responsibility		No Meaningful factor was extracted

TABLE 21 (Cont'd.)

FACTORS (DIMENSIONS) OBTAINED FROM
LIFE STYLE VARIABLES (STATEMENTS)

Extracted Factor Number (Dimension) and Description	Eigen Value and Percent Variance Explained	Life Style Variable (Statement)	Variable Mnemonic	Varimax Factor Loading
		I like to do a lot of partying.	Fash 6	0.369
		I like to go to a beauty parlor as often as I can.	Fash 4	0.353
		I consider it essential for most American families to own a washer and dryer.	Life 4	0.353
FACTOR 4 TELEVISION VIEWING	2.59 (4.9%)	I don't like watching television so I rarely do.	Tel 2	0.799
		Television has added a great deal of enjoyment to my life.	Tel 1	0.788
		I watch television more than I should.	Tel 4	-0.685
		I watch television to be entertained.	Tel. 3	0.486
FACTOR 5 LIFE SIMPLIFICATION PRODUCTS	2.03 (3.8%)	I consider it essential for most American families to own a dishwasher.	Life 2	0.763
		I consider it essential for most American families to own a food disposal unit.	Life 3	0.746

TABLE 21 (Cont'd.)

FACTORS (DIMENSIONS) OBTAINED FROM
LIFE STYLE VARIABLES (STATEMENTS)

Extracted Factor Number (Dimension) and Description	Eigen Value and Percent Variance Explained	Life Style Variable (Statement)	Variable Mnemonic	Varimax Factor Loading
		I consider it essential for most American families to own an automatic coffee maker.	Life 1	0.648
		I consider it essential for most American families to own a washer and dryer.	Life 4	0.486
FACTOR 6 LEISURE WORK ATTITUDE	1.73 (3.3%)	Leisure activities express one's talents better than does a person's job.	Leis 1	0.830
		Leisure activities are more satisfying than a job.	Leis 2	0.821
FACTOR 7 INNOVATIVE BEHAVIOR	1.67 (3.1%)	Sometimes I buy things impulsively and do not feel sorry about it later.	Inn 4	0.669
		I like people who take risks in life without fear of what may happen.	Inn 6	0.553
		I often try new ideas before my friends do.	Inn 1	0.527
		I sometimes influence what my friends say.	Op L 2	0.342
		I feel I am a member of more organizations than most women are.	Inn 3	-0.317

TABLE 21 (Cont'd.)

Extracted Factor Number (Dimension) and Description	Eigen Value and Percent Variance Explained	Life Style Variable (Statement)	Variable Mnemonic	Varimax Factor Loading
FACTOR 8 ACTIVE-LEISURE BEHAVIOR	1.61 (3.0%)	I indulge in sports activities in my free time.	Leis 4	0.739
		It is encouraging to see women participate in outdoors sports as men do.	Leis 5	0.605
		I like to do a lot of partying.	Fash 6	0.553
FACTOR 9 OPINION LEADERSHIP	1.44 (2.7%)	I feel I am a member of more organizations than most women are.	Inn 3	0.583
		I sometimes influence what my friends say.	Op L 2	0.525
		People come to me more often than I go to them for information about brands.	Op L 3	0.523
		At school I volunteered for special projects.	S Res 4	0.481
FACTOR 10 FROZEN FOODS	1.4 (2.6%)	I couldn't get along without frozen foods.	Fr F 1	0.833
		I depend on frozen foods for at least one meal a day.	Fr F 2	0.784

factors which do not lend themselves to rather clear scientific interpretation. Even then the interpretation should be in the nature of a hypothesis
to be sustained, if possible, by subsequent factorial studies." In the following discussion each factor is discussed individually.

Factor 1: Sex Stereotyping

This factor contains seven statements, four of which were previously
grouped under Women's Role in Advertisements and three statements under Toys
and Sex Symbolism. The reason for these two hypothesized dimensions to emerge
as one is that both constructs represent the same basic idea, Sex Stereotyping. An examination of how the three groups fared on individual statements
(see Table 17) reveals that all the seven statements show high degree of significance in the chi-square test. Feminists agreed more strongly than the
other groups that women's roles as depicted in advertisements did not reflect
current reality but were perpetuating stereotyped images. Similarly, in the
case of Toys and Sex Symbolism, equally divergent views between the groups
emerged. Feminists strongly believed in making toys completely non-sexist
while the Traditionalists were strongly opposed to this.

Specifically, the statements that dramatize these differences need some
discussion. One of the items under the hypothesized dimension - Women's Role
in Advertising - is "American advertisements picture a woman's place to be in
the home". Only 38% of the traditionalists agreed with the statement while
64% of the moderates and 89% of the feminists did so. On another statement,
"American advertisements seem to have recognized the changes in women's roles"
48% of the traditionalists, 33% of the moderates and only 22% of the feminists
showed agreement. On a third statement, "American advertisements depict women
as sexual objects", the proportion of traditionalists, moderates and feminists

agreeing were 44%, 56% and 81% respectively. It has been shown by a few researchers that the role portrayals of women in advertisements, over the years, has not changed except very negligibly (Courtney and Lockeretz, 1971; Venkatesan and Losco, 1975).

The hypothesized dimension which brings out the differences between the groups even more vividly is Toys and Sex Symbolism. On one of the three statements, "I would like to see more and more young girls play with mechanical toys", a very small proportion of traditionalists (18%) showed agreement, while 42% of the moderates and 75% of the feminists did so. Similarly, the proportion of respondents agreeing with the statement "I would like to see boys playing with dolls just the way girls do" was 10% in the case of traditionalists, 33% of moderates and 66% of the feminists. Apparently there is less agreement on boys changing their roles than girls changing theirs. Finally, the statement, "Boys and girls should play with the same kind of toys" inspired 30% of traditionalists, 64% of the moderates and 80% of the feminists to agree with it.

Thus, the dimension 'Sex Stereotyping' emerges as the most important dimension in contrasting the views of the three groups. It is not only not surprising that this should be so, but it strengthens the soundness of research in clearly demonstrating the differences between the groups. A further interesting aspect in the formation of this dimension is that not one statement originally listed under the two hypothesized dimensions was left out of the loadings in the extracted factor.

Factor 2: Self-Confidence

In marketing literature, the relationship between Self-confidence and Persuasibility has acquired some importance (Cox and Bauer, 1964; Schuchman

and Perry, 1969) with implications to marketing communications. From psychological literature, it has been suggested that because of the non-agressive
and non-competitive roles of women, Self-confidence has been associated with
masculinity rather than feminity (Bardwick, 1971). In the present analysis,
the factor Self-confidence explained second highest variance. Out of nine
statements included in the hypothesized dimension, seven statements were
clustered into this dimension. The chi-square test on individual statements
does not reveal many differences between groups. However, looking at the frequencies (Table 17), the inescapable fact is that feminists have generally
displayed higher Self-confidence. On six out of nine statements feminists represent the most self-confident group. Joesting (1971), in her study on differences between members and non-members of women's liberation movement, found the
members to be more creative, original and risk-taking. In marketing, the risk-
taking behavior is associated with self-confidence and is an important characteristic of innovators.

Factor 3: Fashion and Personal Appearance

One of the more common dimensions researched in life-style studies, it has
assumed much significance for those involved in female consumer product market.
(Wells, 1974; Tigert, 1973). In a recent review of the history of women's
roles portrayed in various magazine advertisements from 1959-1971, Venkatesan
and Losco (1975) report that women were portrayed more often as being concerned
with physical beauty during 1964-71 than in the previous years. Most recent
criticism of fashion, cosmetic and socially conspicuous products has come from
some feminists who hold that they are a male invention (Ramsey, 1972), that
they are arbitrarily prescribed (Schoolman, 1973) and culturally imposed (Altman, 1973). The reason for including this dimension is to examine its signifi-

cance across the three groups.

The hypothesized dimension contained six statements, all of which show significant loadings in the extracted factor. Two other hypothesized dimensions Self-Confidence and Life Simplification Products have contributed a statement each to this dimension but only one of them (the statement from Self-Confidence), "I would feel extremely uncomfortable if I accidentally went to a formal party in ordinary clothes," really makes some sense in its inclusion. The other statement can be ignored because its loading is the lowest of all the statements.

When one looks at the individual statements, differences between the groups are practically non-existent which probably means that Fashion and Personal Appearance still has same level of importance for women regardless of ideology. About 38% in each group indicated they would like to 'dress smartly'. About 50% in each group stated that they "love to shop for clothes". A large proportion in each group (90%) agreed with the statement "I like to feel attractive". About 60% in each group "enjoy looking through fashion magazines". The results suggests that differences between the groups are negligible and that a large number of women do care a lot about personal appearance.

Factor 4: Television Viewing

The importance of this dimension to marketing communications is obvious from a marketing strategy point of view. Four out of five statements listed under the hypothesized dimension show significant loadings on the extracted factor which does not contain any other statements. On the whole, the attitude toward television viewing as well as the behavior suggest some differences. This is evident from an examination of the statements listed under the hypothe-

sized dimension. Apparently, the views of feminists are less sympathetic to
television viewing than those of other groups. 38% of the traditionalists
admitted that "Television has added a great deal of enjoyment to my life",
while 27% of the moderates and 26% of the feminists did so. Roughly,
equal proportion in each group (50%) watch television "to be entertained".
Those who felt that they watch more television than they should, include
29% traditionalists, 18% moderates and 37% feminists. Those responding to
the statement, "I don't like watching television and so I rarely do", are
24% traditionalists, 37% moderates, 39% feminists. Finally, on the statement which interests marketers most "I don't pay much attention to television
commercials", there were 59% traditionalists, 72% moderates, 71% feminists
showed their agreement.

The statements about television viewing do not reveal any strong positive
or negative feelings, but one can see that the television commercials do not
interest the groups much.

Factor 5: Life Simplification Products

This dimension was included to increase the marketing specificity of the
life-style study. Wells (1972) proposed a paradigm linking consumer characteristics in a continuum that appears as follows:

Demographic Personality Traits	Activities Interests & Opinions	Education of Product Benefits	Preferences	Intentions	Purchases

(Continuum from General to Specific)

As explained earlier, the purpose of this study is not to evaluate product
preferences but to look at the first two cells in the paradigm. However, two
product specific dimensions were included to examine the attitudes of different
groups of women toward a certain class of products. Life simplification products

represent an aspect of the overall life style of an individual because they free up time so that one can engage in other important activities.

The result of the Factor Analysis (Table 20) shows that the extracted factor includes all the statements of the hypothesized dimension. The frequencies on individual statements (Table 17) in the hypothesized dimension show all the groups basically disagreeing that the three products, automatic coffee maker, dishwasher and food disposal unit are essential for most American families. They appear to agree to a large extent that a washer and dryer are essential. However, the traditionalists show a greater appreciation of the need for all the products as a whole than moderates and feminists.

Factor 6: Leisure-Work Attitude
Factor 8: Active-Leisure Behavior

Because these two extracted factors are closely related, they have been combined as a single sub-topic for discussion.

"Leisure' is used in the sense of freedom from work or as 'non-work', while work' is basically remunerative and necessary for family and personal maintenance (Kelley, 1972). The leisure-work paradigm is clearly stated by Noe (1970), Leisure results from the completion of routinized tasks (work) demanded by all social institutions to maintain minimum consensus and order. Since leisure may be defined as activity resulting after the fulfillment of institutional needs -- the resulting leisure may then serve to complement, reinforce, and compensate individuals who normally participate in organized institutions." The implication of this is to be evaluated in terms of how the "relative importance' of work and leisure in a person's life plays in actualizing self-definition Neulinger and Breit, 1971). The inclusion of a leisure-work relationship also has sound sociological basis (de Grazia, 1964; Dumazedier, 1967).

A second aspect of leisure is the manner in which leisure time is used (Fisk, 1963). There is a vast literature in this area but essentially the issue relates to classifying activities on some theoretical basis (Kaplan 1960; de Grazia 1962). Kaplan's classification includes Social; Games and Sport; Art; Movement; Immobility (or Passive). In two studies separated by nearly thirteen years (Havighurst, 1957; Bishop, 1970) leisure activities involving sports and outdoor games showed low or negative correlation in females and high or positive correlation in males. With the advent of feminist movement the female participation in sports and physically demanding activities has aroused much discussion. Accordinging to Shaffer (1972), a medical scientist, "the evidence seems clear that from a constitutional point of view, woman is the stronger sex." Another writer claims "the male's 'overwhelming' superiority of strength and endurance may be more an artifact of social or cultural restriction imposed on the female......than a result of true biological differences in performance potential between the sexes." (Harris, 1972).

Regarding Leisure-Work Attitude the traditionalists seem to favor very slightly, self-definition through leisure, although this difference is not statistically significant. Moderates tend to go with feminists. It is possible that because there are more traditionalists in home-maker roles and fewer of them in career-oriented jobs, their perception of work and leisure differs from members of two other groups.

The other factor relates to leisure activities, and is designated Active-Leisure Behavior as a bipolar construct. One of the statements which shows a high loading on this factor was originally placed under a different hypothe-sized dimension "Fashion and Personal Appearance." But actually it is a state-ment whose meaning suggests leisure behavior "I like to do a lot of partying." Obviously, in the factor analysis the statement found itself under a conceptually more appropriate dimension. In looking at the individual statements and the respective group frequencies, the results reveal some interesting facts. There are significantly more feminists who say that they indulge in sports activities in their free time while the proportion declaring so in the other groups is about the same. Secondly, all groups of women favor female participation in "outdoor sports as men do" but more feminists (96%) and moderates (92%) seem to agree with this situation than traditionalists (78%). The shift from Havighurst's (1957) and Bishop's (1970) findings appears to be partially confirmed.

Factor 7: Innovative Behavior

This dimension has been of considerable significance to marketers in new products decisions (Robertson, 1967, 1971). From a review of various studies, Robertson (1971) concluded that innovative behavior was positively correlated with education, print readership, opinion leadership, income, venturesomeness, attitude toward innovations, social mobility and to some extent with occupational status. It was negatively correlated with perceived risk and brand loyalty. No conclusive relationship was found between innovative behavior and age, television viewership, social participation and generalized self-confidence.

Before any comparison can be made between the groups on Innovative Behavior as a whole, individual statements loading on this factor need to be evaluated. From Table 21, it can be seen that four out of the original six statements showed significant loadings. Also appearing under this factor is an item from Opinion Leadership dimension, "I sometimes influence what my friends say". The proportion of members in each group agreeing with this statement was 33% (traditionalists), 41% (moderates) and 50% (feminists) which seems to show feminists in a favorable light as far as general opinion leadership is concerned. Two state-

ments (under Innovative Behavior) which indicate significant differences
between the groups are, "I often try new ideas before my friends do" and "I
like people who take risks in life without fear of what may happen". Agreeing
with the first one were traditionalists - 49%, moderates - 48%, and feminists -
59%; and with the second one, traditionalists - 34%, moderates - 44%, and
feminists - 51%. The two remaining items, "Sometimes I buy things impulsively
and do not feel sorry about it later", and "I feel I am a member of more organizations than most women are", show no real differences between the groups.

The over all results indicate that feminists are more sympathetic to risk
behavior and are willing to try new ideas. The fact that feminists are also
younger makes them an interesting segment for diffusion researchers. In
general, more feminists than moderates and traditionalists can be classified
as innovators, although this label has not been tested with reference to any
specific product.

Factor 9: Opinion Leadership

In much the same way as Innovative Behavior, Opinion Leadership has been
focus of much attention in diffusion and communication research. In the present study, no differences were found between the groups on individual items
under Opinion Leadership. For example, the proportion of traditionalists,
moderates and feminists agreeing with the statement "My friends or neighbors
often come to me for advice" was 57%, 55%, 58% respectively; with the statement "I sometimes influence what my friends say" it was 33%, 41% and 50% respectively and finally it was 23%, 25% and 18% with the statement "People come
to me more often than I go to them for information about brands". Thus, while
more than fifty percent in each group have been in General Opinion Leadership

roles, only 20% have been in consumer behavior related roles.

Although three statements were included in the hypothesized dimension, only two statements (the latter two) appeared in the entracted factor along with a statement from Innovative Behavior, "I feel I am a member of more organizations than most women are" and a statement from Social Responsibility "At School I volunteered for special projects". Both these statements do refer to overall Leadership construct and, therefore, the extracted factor has been labeled as Opinion Leadership.

An interesting question about opinion leadership is its relationship with innovative behavior. The general impression is that opinion leaders demonstrate greater innovative behavior than their followers but are not necessarily innovators (Robertson and Myers, 1969). In this study, product moment correlations between Opinion Leadership items and Innovative Behavior items were computed. Table 21 shows the results for each individual group as well as for all the groups combined. Generally speaking the correlations between the 6 Innovative Behavior items and 3 Opinion Leadership are low. However, out of a total 18 correlations, feminists represent highest values in ten cases thus indicating that there is stronger association between the opinion leadership and innovative behavior in this group.

Factor 10: Frozen Foods

The two statements included in the hypothesized dimension, "I couldn't get along without frozen foods", and "I depend on frozen food for at least one meal a day" show no differences between the groups. Only a small proportion each agreed with these statements. The extracted factor had both these statements loading on it and no statement from any other dimension appeared. This dimension was included because it was product specific and has the same implications as Life Simplification Products.

TABLE 22 PRODUCT MOMENT CORRELATION BETWEEN

OPINION LEADERSHIP ITEMS AND

INNOVATIVE BEHAVIOR ITEMS

Opinion Leadership Variables

Innovative Behavior (Variables)	Traditionalists			Moderates			Feminists			All Groups Combined		
	Op L1	Op L2	Op L3	Op L1	Op L2	Op L3	Op L1	Op L2	Op L3	Op L2	Op L2	Op L3
Inn 1	.16	.16	.13	.22	.07	.25	.20	.18	.07	.19	.15	.15
Inn 2	.02	-.03	.14	-.09	.20	.25	.21	.18	.14	.05	.10	.17
Inn 3	.09	-.07	.21	.19	.04	.19	.27	.18	.27	.18	.05	.21
Inn 4	-.01	.21	.00	-.01	.11	.00	.09	.10	.00	.02	.14	.00
Inn 5	.26	.05	.17	.21	.00	.06	.16	.16	.12	.21	.06	.12
Inn 6	-.05	.11	.05	-.15	-.05	.03	-.11	-.02	.05	-.10	.04	.04

Explanation:

Innovative Behavior

Inn 1 – I often try new ideas before my friends do.
Inn 2 – When I buy a new brand of product on the shelf, I often buy just to see what it is like.
Inn 3 – I feel I am a member of more organizations than most women are.
Inn 4 – Sometimes I buy things impulsively and do not feel sorry about it later.
Inn 5 – I feel I can talk to most people in the neighborhood any time I feel like it.
Inn 6 – I like people who take risks in life without fear of what may happen.

Opinion Leadership

Op L1 – My friends or neighbors often come to me for advice.
Op L2 – I sometimes influence what my friends say.
Op L3 – People come to me more often than I go to them for information about brands.

In summary, the Factor Analysis captured almost all the hypothesized
imensions except for one, Social Responsibility. The tentative results ap-
ear to be that Feminists are very sensitive to the issue of Sex Stereotyping,
enerally more innovative and much more sympathetic to women participating in
hysically demanding activities. Traditionalists show greater appreciation
or the need for life simplification products, enjoy television viewing and
ave tended to be at the opposite extreme of feminists on various dimensions.
oderates have generally stayed in between traditionalists and feminists.
he groups have not shown any differences on Opinion Leadership, Fashion and
ersonal Appearance.

Analysis of Magazine Readership

In marketing communications, media research includes evaluating vehicle-source effects and locating "media market segments." In a study by Blair (1966), it was revealed that "the attitudes of readers toward a magazine can greatly influence their reaction to advertisements in it." Marc (1966) found that the "degree of involvement" of the reader was a relevant dimension of vehicle-source effect and a method of establishing the involvement is by looking at the regularity of reading on a sematic differential scale (always-never). One of the exhaustive studies in the area of media market segmentation has been carried out by Bass et al (1969), involving 44 magazines and a sample of 344 housewives. Using Factor Analytic procedures they were able to group magazines into five factors, (a) Cultural, Intellectual and Newspapers, (b) Light reading News magazines and Newspapers, (c) Fashion Magazines, (d) Movie, Romance, Crime Magazines and (e) Homemaker Magazines. They also found two dominant population clusters in their sample, the cultural-intellectual cluster and the homemaker cluster. A third cluster was not given any particular label.

In the present study a partial replication of the study of Bass et al (1969) was undertaken with the purpose of evaluating media reading habits of the three groups of women. A total of 34 magazines were selected (see page 3 of the questionnaire for complete list). Against each magazine, the respondent was asked to indicate regularity of reading on a five-point scale, "I Never Read It," "I Occasionally Read It," "I Read About Half Issues," "I Read About Two of Every Three Issues," "I Read Almost Every Issue." These categories were assigned numerical values of 1,2,3,4 and 5 respectively as in Likert type summated rating scale.

Table 23 compares the factors extracted in this study with the results of the study by Bass et al (1969). Table 24 gives detailed results of the Factor analysis along with the proportion of women in each group who read the magazines that are loaded on each factor. Table 25 shows all magazines that showed statistically significant differences between the groups in their reported reading habits. Table 26 shows all magazines which do not reveal any such differences. Finally, Table 27 lists the magazines in a rank order of readership for each group. A person is said to "read the magazine" if she responds to any one of the three response categories, "I Read About Half the Issues", "I Read About Two of Every Three Issues", and "I Read Almost Every Issue". Thus, these three categories represent "regularity of reading construct".

Factor Analysis of Magazines

A Factor analysis was performed on all 34 magazines using the combined data of the three groups. The magazines which were grouped under seven factors were compared (Table 23) to the factors reported by Bass et al (1969). The factors extracted in both studies are comparable in terms of the magazine groupings. Four of the five factors reported in the study by Bass et al have appeared in the present study with almost the same magazines. There is no factor in the present study corresponding to their "light reading." The two factors from the present study "National and International News" and "Business and Consumer Magazines" have no corresponding factors in their study which found the national newspaper New York Times (Daily and Sunday) loading heavily on 'Cultural, Intellectual' factor.

The Factor analysis resulted in natural groupings of magazines (Table 24). However, two of the twenty-nine magazines which had significant loadings on the

factors, appeared under two factors. For example, the feminist magazine Ms.
appeared both under "National and International News" and "Cultural, Intellectual
Magazines". Similarly, the commercial weekly Business Week appeared both under
"Business and Consumer Magazines" and "Local News". Two other magazines which
looked somewhat misplaced were T.V. Guide which was associated with "Fashion
Magazines" and U.S. News and World which loaded on "Cultural, Intellectual
Magazines" factor. But for these minor exceptions, the Factor analysis gave a
very good fit. Five magazines that failed to load significantly on any of the
seven factors were Reader's Digest, TIME, National Geographic, Sports Illustrated
and Esquire. It is interesting to note that TIME magazine ranked the highest
among the magazines read by Feminists while Reader's Digest ranked third among
the magazines read by traditionalists and moderates (Table 27).

The pattern of reading habits shows some differences between the groups.
Magazines clustered around 'Homemaker Magazines' factor show significant differences between the groups. Traditionalists and moderates account for a large
readership of these magazines with feminists showing low values.

In the case of 'National and International News' Factor the magazines
loading on this factor appear to draw most of their readership from feminists
groups. The individual magazines reveal some significant differences.

As for 'Local News' factor, traditionalists account for largest readership,
although in general all the groups indicate high level of readership. The
individual magazines reveal some differences between the groups.

In the case of 'Cultural, Intellectual Magazines' Factor, the one magazine
which shows significant differences is Ms. which is read practically by feminists
only. Generally, the readership of these magazines across the groups is rather
low, with traditionalists showing no interest in them at all.

TABLE 23. MAGAZINE READERSHIP

FACTOR COMPARISON

Factors Extracted in this Study (Factor Number in Parenthesis)	Corresponding Factors in Bass et al (1969) (Factor Number in Parenthesis)
Homemaker Magazines (Factor 1) (Family Circle, Woman's Day, Better Homes and Gardens, Good Housekeeping, McCall's, Home Beautiful)	Homemaker Magazines (Factor 5) (Family Circle, Woman's Day, Better Homes and Gardens, Good Housekeeping, Ladies' Home Journal, Better Homes and Gardens)
Movie, Romance Magazines (Factor 2) (True Story, Modern Romance, True Confessions, Modern Screen)	Movie, Romance Magazines (Factor 4) (Modern Romance, True Story, True Confessions, Modern Screen)
National and International News (Factor 3) (New York Times (Sunday), New York Times (Daily), News Week, Ms.)	(No corresponding factor reported. Newspapers were included in Cultural, Intellectual Factor)
Business and Consumer Magazines (Factor 4) (Consumer Bulletin, Consumer Reports, Business Week)	(No corresponding factor reported)
Fashion Magazines (Factor 5) (Cosmopolitan, Glamour, T.V. Guide)	Fashion Magazines (Factor 3) (Vogue, Harper's Bazaar, Glamour, Mademoiselle, House Beautiful, Holiday)
Cultural, Intellectual Magazines (Factor 6) (Saturday Review, New Yorker, Harpers, U.S. News & World, Atlantic Monthly, Ms.)	Cultural, Intellectual Magazines (Factor 1) (New York Times (Daily), New York Times (Sunday), Saturday Review, New Yorker, Atlantic Monthly, Consumer Reports, Esquire)
Local News (Factor 7) (Syracuse Post (Standard), Syracuse Herald Journal, Business Week)	Light Reading (Factor 2) (Post, Reader's Digest, Indianapolis Star, Look, Ladies' Home Journal, Life)

TABLE 24. — FACTOR ANALYSIS OF MAGAZINE READERSHIP

Factor Number and Description	Eigen Value and Contribution to Variance	Magazine Included in Each Factor	Factor Loading	Number of Women In Each Group Who Tend to Read the Magazine			Significance Level of Chi-Square Value	Remarks
				Traditionalists (%)	Moderates (%)	Feminists (%)		
Factor 1 Home Maker Magazines	5.26 (15.5%)	Family Circle	0.861	33	43	21	0.0600	a) More Moderates and Traditionalists read these than Feminists b) More Moderates read these than Traditionalists
		Woman's Day	0.823	32	39	22	0.0279	
		Better Homes and Gardens	0.726	29	30	13	0.0010	
		Good Housekeeping	0.691	34	29	12	0.0070	
		McCalls	0.459	16	22	12	0.0482	
		House Beautiful	0.423	7	6	8	NS	
Factor 2 Movie, Romance Magazines (Sensationalistic)	3.54 (10.4%)	True Story	0.914	3	2	1	NS	a) Practically read by none in any of the groups b) Least read magazines
		Modern Romance	0.909	5	0	1	0.04	
		True Confessions	0.899	3	3	1	NS	
		Modern Romance	0.658	3	0	1	NS	
Factor 3 National and International News	2.66 (7.8%)	New York Times (Sunday)	0.811	7	22	33	0.0001	a) More Feminists read these than Moderates or Traditionalists b) More Moderates read these than Traditionalists
		New York Times (Daily)	0.758	5	9	22	0.0000	
		Newsweek	0.529	22	30	49	0.0045	
		Ms.	0.400	1	10	22	0.0000	
Factor 4 Business and Consumer Magazines	1.72 (5.1%)	Consumer Bulletin	0.765	6	11	8	NS	a) About the same level of readership in all groups
		Consumer Reports	0.704	13	22	22	NS	
		Business Week	0.478	5	4	6	NS	
Factor 5 Fashion Magazines	1.5 (4.4%)	Cosmopolitan	0.744	13	16	19	NS	a) About the same level of readership in all groups
		Glamour	0.678	14	15	14	NS	
		T.V. Guide	0.374	23	21	21	NS	
Factor 6 Cultural, Intellectual Magazines	1.23 (3.6%)	Saturday Review	0.785	1	3	6	0.2000	a) Traditionalists show low readership; Moderates and Feminists significantly higher in readership
		New Yorker	0.709	1	15	14	0.0000	
		Harpers	0.566	4	6	6	NS	
		U.S. News & World Report	0.393	8	9	7	NS	
		Atlantic Monthly	0.369	1	6	3	0.330	
		Ms.	0.325	1	10	22	0.0000	
Factor 7 Local News	1.02 (3.0%)	Syracuse Post - Standard	0.728	41	32	26	NS	a) Local News readership high among groups b) But it is much more among Traditionalists
		Syracuse Herald Journal	0.403	67	64	46	0.0000	
		Business Week	0.360	5	4	6	NS	

MAGAZINE READERSHIP OF GROUPS

(Cell Values Show Number of Women in Each Group
Who Tend to Read the Magazine)

Magazines Which Show Significant
Differences Across the Groups

Magazine	Traditionalists Who Tend to Read the Magazine N = 111	Moderates Who Tend to Read the Magazine N = 109	Feminists Who Tend to Read the Magazine N = 113	Total Who Tend to Read the Magazine N = 333	Significance Level of Chi-Square Value
Syracuse Herald Journal	74 (67)*	70 (64)	52 (46)	196 (59)	0.0300
Time	27 (24)	39 (36)	56 (50)	112 (34)	0.0028
News Week	24 (22)	33 (30)	55 (49)	112 (34)	0.0045
Family Circle	37 (33)	47 (43)	24 (21)	108 (32)	0.0600
Reader's Digest	38 (34)	42 (39)	21 (19)	101 (30)	0.0043
Woman's Day	34 (32)	42 (39)	25 (22)	101 (30)	0.0279
Good Housekeeping	38 (34)	31 (29)	14 (12)	83 (25)	0.0070
Better Homes and Gardens	32 (29)	33 (30)	15 (13)	80 (24)	0.0010
New York Times Weekly	8 (7)	24 (22)	37 (33)	69 (27)	0.0001
McCalls	18 (16)	24 (22)	13 (12)	45 (17)	0.0482
New York Times Daily	5 (5)	10 (9)	24 (22)	39 (12)	0.0000
Ms.	1 (1)	11 (10)	24 (22)	36 (11)	0.0000

(* Figures in Parenthesis are percentages
rounded off.)

Table 25 (Cont'd.)

Magazine	Traditionalists Who Tend to Read the Magazine N = 111	Moderates Who Tend to Read the Magazine N = 109	Feminists Who Tend to Read the Magazine N = 113	Total Who Tend to Read the Magazine N = 333	Significance Level of Chi-Square Value
New Yorker	1 (1)	15 (13)	14 (12)	30 (9)	0.0006
Esquire	3 (3)	6 (6)	7 (6)	16 (5)	0.0400
Saturday Review	1 (1)	3 (3)	7 (6)	11 (3)	0.0200
Atlantic Monthly	1 (1)	1 (1)	7 (6)	9 (3)	0.0330
Modern Romance	5 (5)	0 (0)	1 (1)	6 (2)	0.0400

TABLE 26

MAGAZINE READERSHIP OF GROUPS

(Cell Values Show Number of Women in Each Group
Who Tend to Read the Magazine)

Magazines Which Show No Significant[a]
Differences Across the Groups

Magazines from Most to Least Read	Traditionalists Who Tend to Read the Magazine N = 111	Moderates Who Tend to Read the Magazine N = 109	Feminists Who Tend to Read the Magazine N = 113	Total Who Tend to Read the Magazine N = 333
Syracuse Post Standard	46 (41)[b]	38 (32)	29 (26)	113 (34)
National Geographic	23 (22)	26 (24)	35 (31)	87 (26)
T.V. Guide	25 (23)	23 (21)	23 (21)	71 (21)
Consumer Reports	14 (13)	24 (22)	24 (22)	62 (19)
Cosmopolitan	14 (13)	17 (16)	21 (19)	52 (16)
Glamour	15 (14)	16 (15)	15 (14)	46 (14)
Consumer Bulletin	7 (6)	12 (11)	9 (8)	28 (9)
U.S. News and World Report	9 (8)	10 (9)	8 (7)	27 (8)
Sports Illustrated	10 (9)	10 (9)	6 (6)	26 (8)

a. Based on Chi-Square test using contingency tables.

b. Percent figures in parenthesis are rounded off.

Table 26 (Cont'd.)

Magazines from Most to Least Read	Traditionalists Who Tend to Read the Magazine N = 111	Moderates Who Tend to Read the Magazine N = 109	Feminists Who Tend to Read the Magazine N = 113	Total Who Tend to Read the Magazine N = 333
House Beautiful	8 (7)	6 (6)	9 (8)	23 (7)
Business Week	5 (5)	4 (4)	6 (6)	15 (5)
Harper's	4 (4)	3 (3)	6 (6)	13 (4)
Holiday	3 (3)	2 (2)	2 (2)	7 (2)
True Confessions	3 (3)	3 (3)	1 (1)	7 (2)
Field and Stream	1 (1)	2 (2)	3 (3)	6 (2)
True Story	3 (3)	2 (2)	1 (1)	6 (2)
Modern Screen	3 (3)	0 (0)	1 (1)	4 (1)

TABLE 27. RANKING OF MAGAZINES FROM MOST READ TO LEAST READ

Traditionalists (N = 111)

Rank	Magazine	%
1	Syracuse Herald Journal	(67)*
2	Syracuse Post Standard	(41)
3.5	Reader's Digest	(34)
3.5	Good Housekeeping	(34)
5	Family Circle	(33)
6	Woman's Day	(32)
7	Better Homes & Gardens	(29)
8	TIME	(24)
9	T.V. Guide	(23)
10.5	National Geographic	(22)
10.5	Newsweek	(22)
12	McCall's	(16)
13	Glamour	(14)
14.5	Cosmopolitan	(13)
14.5	Consumer Reports	(13)
16	Sports Illustrated	(9)
17	U.S. News & World Report	(8)
18.5	House Beautiful	(7)
18.5	New York Times (Sunday)	(7)
20	Consumer Bulletin	(6)
21	Business Week	(5)
22	New York Times (Daily)	(5)
22	Modern Romance	(5)
24	Harper's	(4)
27	Holiday	(3)
27	Esquire	(3)
27	True Confessions	(3)
27	True Story	(3)
27	Modern Screen	(3)
28	Field and Stream	(1)
28	Atlantic Monthly	(1)
28	Saturday Review	(1)
28	New Yorker	(1)
28	Ms.	(1)

Moderates (N = 109)

Rank	Magazine	%
1	Syracuse Herald Journal	(66)
2	Family Circle	(43)
3.5	Reader's Digest	(34)
3.5	Women's Day	(34)
5	TIME	(32)
6	Syracuse Post Standard	(30)
7.5	Newsweek	(30)
7.5	Better Homes & Gardens	(24)
9	Good Housekeeping	(23)
10	National Geographic	(22)
12	Consumer Reports	(22)
12	New York Times (Sunday)	(22)
14	McCall's	(16)
14	T.V. Guide	(14)
15	Cosmopolitan	(13)
16	Glamour	(13)
17	New Yorker	(9)
18	Consumer Bulletins	(8)
19	Ms.	(7)
21	New York Times (Daily)	(6)
21	U.S. News & World Report	(6)
21	Sports Illustrated	(6)
23.5	House Beautiful	(5)
23.5	Esquire	(5)
25	Business Week	(4)
27	Harper's	(3)
27	Saturday Review	(3)
27	True Confessions	(3)
30	Holiday	(2)
30	Field and Stream	(2)
30	True Story	(1)
32	Atlantic Monthly	(1)
33	Modern Romance	(0)
34	Modern Screen	(0)

Feminists (N = 113)

Rank	Magazine	%
1	TIME	(50)
2	Newsweek	(49)
3	Syracuse Herald Journal	(46)
4	New York Times (Sunday)	(33)
5	National Geographic	(31)
6	Syracuse Post Standard	(26)
8.5	Ms.	(22)
8.5	New York Times (Daily)	(22)
8.5	Woman's Day	(22)
8.5	Consumer Reports	(21)
11.5	T.V. Guide	(21)
11.5	Family Circle	(21)
13.5	Cosmopolitan	(19)
13.5	Reader's Digest	(19)
15	Glamour	(14)
16	Better Homes & Gardens	(13)
18	Good Housekeeping	(12)
18	McCall's	(12)
18	New Yorker	(12)
20.5	Consumer Bulletin	(9)
20.5	House Beautiful	(9)
22	U.S. News and World Report	(7)
25.5	Sports Illustrated	(6)
25.5	Saturday Review	(6)
25.5	Atlantic Monthly	(6)
25.5	Harper's	(6)
25.5	Business Week	(6)
29	Field and Stream	(3)
30.5	Holiday	(2)
30.5	True Confessions	(2)
33	True Story	(1)
33	Modern Screen	(1)

All Groups (N = 333)

Rank	Magazine	%
1	Syracuse Herald Journal	(59)
3	Syracuse Post Standard	(34)
3	TIME	(34)
3	Newsweek	(34)
5	Family Circle	(32)
6.5	Reader's Digest	(30)
6.5	Woman's Day	(30)
10	Better Homes & Gardens	(24)
11.5	New York Times (Weekly)	(21)
11.5	T.V. Guide	(21)
13	Consumer Reports	(19)
14	McCall's	(17)
15	Cosmopolitan	(16)
16	Glamour	(14)
17	New York Times (Daily)	(12)
18	Ms.	(11)
19.5	New Yorker	(9)
19.5	Consumer Bulletin	(9)
21.5	U.S. News and World Report	(8)
21.5	Sports Illustrated	(8)
23	House Beautiful	(7)
26.5	Business Week	(5)
26.5	Esquire	(5)
26	Harper's	(4)
27.5	Atlantic Monthly	(3)
27.5	Saturday Review	(3)
31	Holiday	(2)
31	True Confessions	(2)
31	Field and Stream	(2)
31	True Story	(2)
31	Modern Romance	(2)
34	Modern Screen	(1)

*Figures in parenthesis represent per cent in each group who tend to read the magazine.

There are no significant differences between the groups on magazines which
are loaded on three factors, 'Fashion Magazines,' which have above average
readership among the groups; 'Business and Consumer magazines' which show below
average readership; and 'Movie, Romance Magazines' which have practically no
readership among the groups.

Ranking of Magazines

One of the results of the analysis is the ranking of magazines from "most-
read" to "least read" by each group as well as for the entire sample (Table 27).

For the entire sample, it can be seen that the frequency of reading is
highest in the case of Local News, followed by National and International News
(TIME and Newsweek), Light Reading and Home Maker magazines (Reader's Digest,
Family Circle, etc.), Cultural, Intellectual magazines (Harper's, etc.), and
Movie, Romance magazines (True Story, etc.).

For each group, however, the pattern varies. The major differences between
the groups in individual magazine rankings are seen in the following magazines.

Readership Ranking Among

Magazine	Traditionalists	Moderates	Feminists
Reader's Digest	3.5	3.5	13.5
Good Housekeeping	5	9	18
Family Circle	5	9	18
Better Homes and Gardens	7	7.5	16
TIME	8	5	1
News Week	10.5	7	2
McCall's	12	12	18
New York Times (Sunday)	18.5	12	4
New York Times (Daily)	22	21	8.5
Ms.	28	19	8.5

Reader's Digest is one of the most establishment oriented or "Middle
erican" magazines. It has high readership among traditionalists and moderates
t much lower ranking among feminists. Homemaker magazines reveal fairly
gh readership among traditionalists but low readership among feminists. How-
er, TIME and Newsweek rank the highest among feminists and New York Times
unday and Daily) is close at the top. These occupy rather low positions
long traditionalists and moderates. The most glaring difference is observed in
e case of Ms., a recent magazine that reflects the current thinking of
eminists. It has practically no readership among traditionalists but a
bstantial readership among feminists with moderates exactly half way between
eminists and traditionalists.

To summarize, the magazine reading habits of the three groups differ
nsiderably with traditionalists and feminists somewhat at the opposite extremes
nd the moderates in the middle. The overall readership pattern of moderates
ppears to be closer to traditionalists more than the feminists. Feminists show
igher readership of magazines that have National and International news value
hile moderates and traditionalists tend to read Home Maker magazines. All the
roups show relatively low interest in Cultural, Intellectual magazines. An
mpressive result of the Factor analysis is the formation of natural groupings of
agazines and a general agreement with a previous study by Bass et al (1969).

Discriminant Analysis[*] of Life
Style and Demographic Variables

The purpose in using a discriminant procedure was to evaluate the group differences with all variables simultaneously in the model. The stepwise multi-discriminant analysis retains only those variables which are found significant and drops the others. The discriminant procedure identifies the discriminant function or functions which are significant and proceeds to classify individuals into groups to demonstrate its predictive efficacy.

The input data to the discriminant analysis consisted of factor scores derived from the factor analysis (combined group) of life style variables and measures on demographic characteristics. A total of 18 variables entered the analysis. The sample was divided into two random halves so that one half of the sample could be used for discriminant analysis and the other half as a validating sample for classification purpose. This makes classification free of bias because the same sample used to estimate the discriminant coefficients should not be used for classification or prediction of new members. (Frank, et al 1965). Accordingly, a sample of 55 respondents from each group was selected for a total of 165 for the discriminant analysis. The remaining 168 respondents constituted the validating sample.

Table 28 presents the uni-variate F-ratios of life style and demographic variables which entered the discriminant analysis. The significant variables are (1) Sex Stereotyping, (2) Life Simplification Products, (3) Household Status, (4) Religion, (5) Age, and (6) Education. Not surprisingly, the variable 'Sex Stereotyping' emerged as the most significant variable in terms of the F-value.

Two discriminant functions were obtained from the analysis as shown in Table 29. Only the first function is significant and its eigenvalue is 0.659 with a

---

* See Appendix 4 for a theoretical discussion of Multiple Discriminant Analysis.

TABLE 28 DISCRIMINANT ANALYSIS

(Life Style and Demographic Variables)

Means and Univariate F - Ratios of Discriminant Variables

Variable	Traditionalists	Moderates	Feminists	All Groups	Uni-Variate F-Ratio
Sex Stereotyping	0.5875	0.1651	-0.7275	0.0048	36.9441***
Self-Confidence	-0.0573	0.0532	0.1580	0.0520	0.6633
Fashion-Behavior	-0.0478	0.1421	-0.0451	0.0168	0.7709
Television Viewing	0.0515	-0.1423	0.0706	-0.0071	0.7099
Life-Simplifying Products	0.2230	-0.3057	0.0029	-0.0281	4.1307*
Leisure-Work Attitude	0.0692	0.0385	0.0693	0.0589	0.0184
Innovative Behavior	-0.1763	0.0302	-0.0329	-0.0589	0.5847
Active-Leisure Behavior	-0.2015	0.0077	0.2136	0.0079	2.3693
Opinion Leadership	-0.0386	-0.0563	0.0034	-0.0304	0.0558
	0.0816	0.0121	0.0474	0.0468	0.0585
Marital Status	1.9444	2.3636	1.8727	2.0610	1.3946
Work Status	3.6852	2.8909	3.0545	3.2073	2.0152
Household Status	3.0185	3.0264	3.5455	3.2012	3.8624*
Religion	1.6667	2.1273	2.1818	1.9939	3.4980*
Race	1.2037	1.1818	1.2182	1.2012	0.0292
Age	2.8704	2.3091	2.1636	2.4451	3.6781*
Education	4.1296	4.4182	4.8545	4.4695	6.4899**
Income	3.6481	3.3636	3.3455	3.4512	0.5171

F-Ratio with 2 and 161 degrees of freedom

(*** Significant at 0.0000 level)
(** Significant at 0.01 level)
(* Significant at 0.05 14v41)

TABLE 29 DISCRIMINANT FUNCTION COEFFICIENTS

(Life Style and Demographic Variables)

Variable	Order of Entry	Relative Importance	Discriminant Function 1		Discriminant Function 2	
			Standardized Coefficients	Unstandardized Coefficients	Standardized Coefficients	Unstandardized Coefficients
Constant				-0.336		0.361
Sex Stereotyping	1	1	-0.834	-0.851	-0.095	-0.097
Self-Confidence	5	4	0.204	0.209	0.038	0.039
Fashion Behavior	7	7	-0.059	-0.065	-0.410	-0.448
Television Viewing						
Life Simplification Products	2	8	-0.035	-0.036	0.795	0.809
Leisure-Work Attitude						
Innovative Behavior						
Active-Leisure Behavior	8	6	0.150	0.149	0.005	-0.005
Opinion Leadership						
Frozen Foods						
Marital Status	6	5	-0.175	-0.105	-0.390	-0.234
Work Status						
Household Status						
Religion						
Race						
Age	3	2	-0.248	-0.170	0.155	0.106
Education	4	3	0.235	0.215	-0.027	-0.025
Income						

elative percentage contribution of 88.96 as compared to 11.04% of the second
unction. The chi-square value for the first function is 92.074 (16 df) and for
he second function it is 12.373 (7 df).(Table 30).

A more graphic way of evaluating them is by looking at the group centroids.
n the first discriminant function the group centroids are -0.688, -0.154 and
.830 for traditionalists, moderates and feminists respectively. On the second
iscriminant function the group centroids are 0.251, -0.380 and 0.134 respec-
ively. The first function clearly separates the three groups with tradition-
lists and feminists at the extreme positions and the moderates in the middle
lthough a little closer to the traditionalists. The second function brings the
roups much closer and when compared to the first function,
istinguishable.

The group centroids on the two dimensions* are shown in Figure 5 on the
ollowing page.

Table 29 presents the order of entry of variables and their relative importance. According to order of entry the variables which entered the analysis are
(1) Sex Stereotyping, (2) Life Simplification Products, (3) Age, (4) Education,
(5) Self-Confidence, (6) Marital Status, (7) Fashion Behavior and (8) Active-
Leisure Behavior. These are the only variables which were retained in the analysis. The remaining 10 variables were dropped. Two variables, Household Status
and Religion which were found significant in the Uni-variate F-test were not included in the discriminant set.

The relative importance of individual variables is perhaps more meaningful
in discriminant analysis. Their relative importance is indicated by the absolute
magnitude of the standardized coefficients of the variables in the first discriminant function. According to the relative magnitude of the coefficients (ignoring

---

*In the latter analysis, the second discriminant function is left out from
discussion.

FIGURE 5. DISCRIMINANT ANALYSIS LIFESTYLE AND DEMOGRAPHIC VARIABLES

DISCRIMINANT SCORE 1 (HORIZONTAL) VS. DISCRIMINANT SCORE 2 (VERTICAL)

GROUP CENTROIDS T*(TRADITIONAL), M*(MODERATE), F*(FEMINIST).

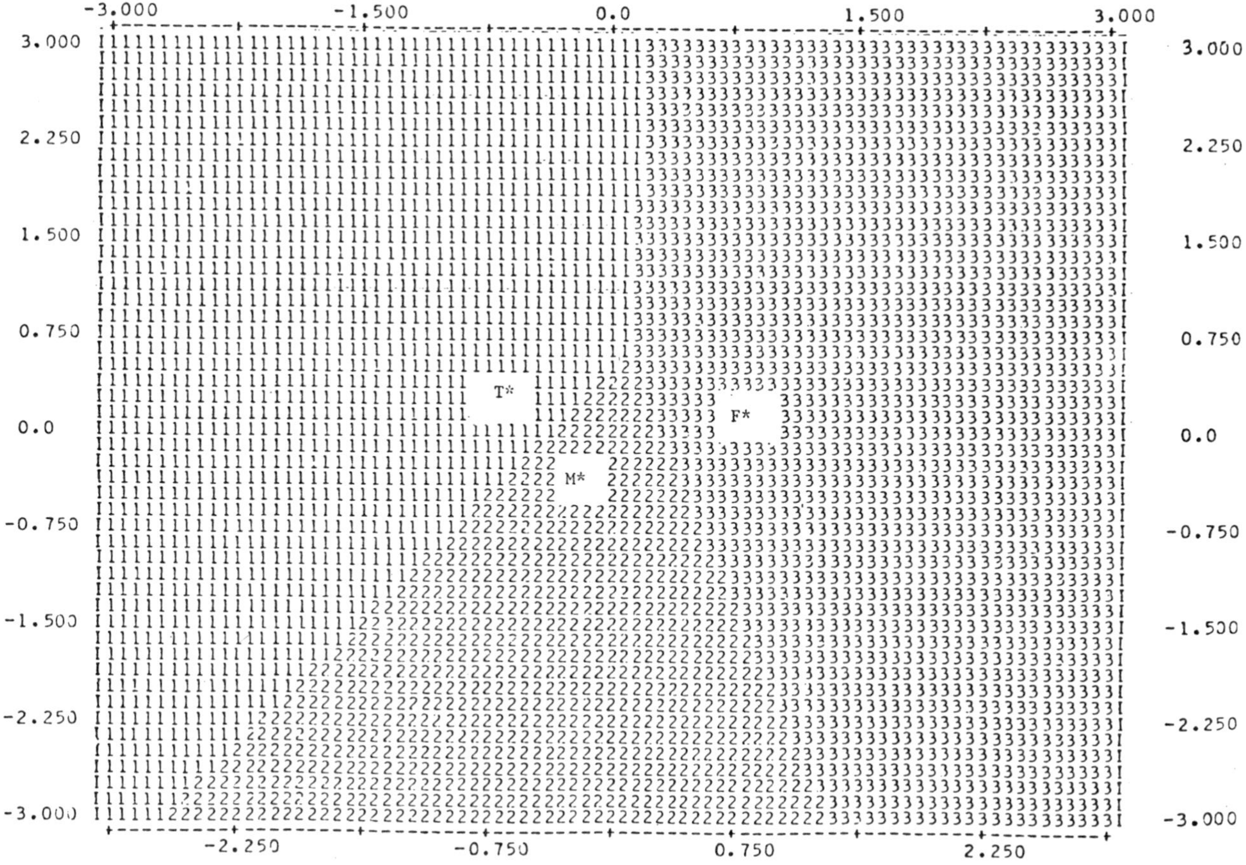

ieir signs), the discriminant variables are (1) Sex Stereotyping, (2) Age, (3) Jucation, (4) Self-Confidence, (5) Marital Status, (6) Active-Leisure Behavior, 7) Fashion Behavior and (8) Life Simplification Products. The three most important variables in terms of their discriminating ability are Sex Stereotyping, ge and Education. This confirms the earlier findings and thus the procedure an be considered a validating check. The least important variables are Fashion ehavior and Life Simplification products which suggests that there are only arginal differences between the groups with respect to marketing specific actors. The three other variables which are of middle range importance are elf-Confidence and Active-Leisure Behavior, which in the earlier analysis reealed some differences between the groups but not to the same extent as Sex tereotyping, Age and Education. A surprise inclusion in the discriminant set as 'Marital Status,' a variable which revealed no significant differences etween the groups in the chi-square analysis. As for the variables which were ropped from the discriminant set, there are a few surprises. The demographic ariables Work Status, Household Status and Religion earlier showed significant ifferences between the groups in the chi-square test (Tables 14, 15 and 16). ut these demographic variables found no place in the discriminant set. The ife style variables not included in the discriminant model are Television Viewing, esiure-Work Attitude, Innovative Behavior, Opinion Leadership and Frozen Foods, hich confirms earlier finding that individual statements on these dimensions ring out relatively minor differences between the groups.

The next major question in the discriminant analysis is how to classify as et "unlabeled" individuals into one or another of the three groups. The classi- ication procedure can be strengthened by taking prior probabilities into con- ideration. In the present study, the groups in the sample are almost equal in ize with traditionalists - 111, moderates - 109 and feminists - 113. Thus, the

TABLE 30 DISCRIMINANT ANALYSIS

(Life Style and Demographic Variables)

	Function 1	Function 2
Group Centroids:		
Traditionalists	-0.688	0.251
Moderates	-0.154	-0.380
Feminists	0.830	0.134
Eigen Value	0.659	0.082
Relative Percentage	88.96	11.04
Canonical Correlation	0.630	0.275
Wilks' Lambda	0.5573	0.9244
Chi-Square	92.074	12.373
Degrees of Freedom	16	7
Significance	0.000	0.089

rior probability for each group was set equal to 0.33 which means that an

ndividual selected at random from a mixed population comprising all three

roups, has an equal probability of being a member of any one of the groups.

he procedure uses an assignment rule for classifying individuals.

Table 31 presents the prediction results using both the original sample

which was used to generate the discriminant function) and the validating sample.

lthough it is the validating sample that really matters, the original sample

as been presented for comparison purposes. Using the original sample the

iscriminant function correctly classified 63% of the traditionalists, 47.3%

f the moderates and 81.8% of feminists. Using the validating sample it cor-

ectly classified 60.7% of the traditionalists, 35.2% of the moderates and 72.4%

f the feminists. The classification is very satisfactory as far as tradition-

lists and feminists are concerned, although the classification of moderates

s not so. The result is not very surprising because the moderates being the

middle group, they do reveal some characteristics of both the other groups.

This is evident from the fact that 37% of the moderates are classified as tra-

ditionalists and 28% as feminists. The results would have been more discouraging

nad the incorrectly classified moderates been assigned to either of the two

ther groups because their assumed position was in the middle of a continuum.

here, however seems to be a slight inclination for moderates to be allied with

the traditionalists rather than the feminists. For example, more moderates are

lassified as traditionalists (37%) than feminists (27.8%). Similarly, more

traditionalists (35.7%) are classified as moderates than feminists (20.7%).

This difference is not statistically tested but yet provides an interesting in-

sight into the analysis. The two extreme groups appear to have very little in

common with each other with only 3.6% of the traditionalists classified as femi-

nists as traditionalists.

TABLE 31 DISCRIMINANT ANALYSIS - CLASSIFICATION

(Life Style and Demographic Variables)

Prediction Results - With Original Sample

Actual Group	No. of Cases	Predicted Group Membership		
		Group 1	Group 2	Group 3
1 (Traditionalists)	54.	34. 63.0%	15. 27.8%	5. 9.3%
2 (Moderates)	55.	14. 25.5%	26. 47.3%	15. 27.3%
3 (Feminists)	55.	5. 9.1%	5. 9.1%	45. 81.8%

Prediction Results - With Validating Sample

Actual Group	No. of Cases	Predicted Group Membership		
		Group 1	Group 2	Group 3
1 (Traditionalists)	56	34 60.7%	20 35.7%	2 3.6%
2 (Moderates)	54	20 37%	19 35.2%	15 27.8%
3 (Feminists)	58	4 6.9%	12 20.7%	42 72.4%

To answer the question as to how much better than chance did the discriminant function do, one has to compare the predicted results with prior probabilities. The probability that an individual would be assigned to any of the groups on the basis of chance is 0.33. But the discriminant function shows that it is capable of doing considerably better than chance, a little better than twice in the case of feminists, just a little worse than twice in the case of traditionalists and about the same in the case of moderates. Thus the overall result is impressive.

The overall significance of the discriminant analysis lies in its ability to evaluate the group differences with the simultaneous inclusion of all the variables in the model. Since this technique is very powerful, it makes the results much more meaningful. The analysis has revealed significant group differences on the basis of certain life style and demographic variables thus confirming what appeared to be tentative results in the earlier discussion.

Some Limitations in the use of Discriminant Analysis

One of the assumptions of the linear discriminant model is that of equal variance and covariance matrix. There is a test for equality of group covariance matrices called the 'Box's M' and its associated F test. This test was not included in the SPSS program available in the computing center and consequently the assumption was not validated.

Another assumption that was violated relates to the nature of the independent variables which in the discriminant model are assumed to be normal and continuous. Obviously some of the demographic variables did not fit this description and to this extent the results must be carefully interpreted.

Discriminant Analysis of
Magazine Readership Factors

A step-wise discriminant analysis was performed to evaluate the discriminating ability of the linear combination of magazine factors. The input to
discriminant analysis were the factor scores obtained from the factor analysis
of magazine variables. Since each group membership in the sample was almost
equal, the prior probability of group membership was set equal to 0.33. Half
the sample in each group was used to generate the discriminant function and
the other half as the validating sample for prediction of new group membership.
The results are presented in Tables 32 thru 35.

The Uni-variate F-ratios (Table 32) indicate highly significant differences
on two factors, Homemaker, Magazines and National and International News and
low significance on Business and Consumer Magazines and Local News. The other
factors reveal no differences at all between the groups.

Table 33 presents the order in which the discriminating variables entered
in the step-wise procedure. Out of the eight variables entered in the analysis,
all but one were retained. The only variable which was left out was "Cultural,
Intellectual Magazines" Factor which is rather surprising because, in an earlier
analysis of individual magazines, this factor appeared to differentiate the
groups better than the magazines that loaded on three other factors, Fashion
Magazines, Business and Consumer Magazines and Movie, Romance Magazines (See
Table 24). In order of entry, the included discriminant variables were (1)
Homemaker Magazines, (2) International News, (3) Local News, (4) Movie,
Romance Magazines, (5) Fashion Magazines, and (6) Business and Consumer Maga-
zines.

A more important result than the order of entry of variables is the magnitude of standardized coefficients. In the order of their relative magnitude

TABLE 32 DISCRIMINANT ANALYSIS

(Magazine Readership)

(Means and Univariate F-Ratios of Discriminant Variables)

Variable	Traditionalists	Moderates	Feminists	All Groups	Uni-Variate F-Ratio
Homemaker Magazines	0.1805	0.4411	-0.4361	0.0618	12.8227**
Movie, Romance Magazines	0.0908	0.1015	-0.1735	0.0061	1.6399
National and International News	-0.3053	-0.0651	0.3899	0.0065	7.4608**
Business and Consumer Magazines	-0.1109	-0.0021	0.2076	0.0315	1.2951
Fashion Magazines	-0.1862	0.1859	-0.1553	-0.0519	2.7610*
Cultural, Intellectual Magazines	-0.1933	-0.0316	0.0867	-0.0461	1.0406
Local News	0.1696	-0.0146	-0.2558	-0.0336	2.5669*

F-Ratio with 2 and 162 Degrees of Freedom

**Highly Significant

*Significant at 0.10 Level

TABLE 33 DISCRIMINANT FUNCTION COEFFICIENTS

(Magazine Readership)

	Order of Entry	Relative Importance	Discriminant Function 1		Discriminant Function 2	
			Standardized Coefficients	Unstandardized Coefficients	Standardized Coefficients	Understandardized Coefficients
Constant	–	–	–	-0.0130	–	-0.0142
Homemaker Magazines	1	1	0.6312	0.6324	0.4694	0.4703
Movie, Romance Magazines	4	3	0.3433	0.3794	-0.0810	-0.0896
National and International News	2	2	-0.5867	-0.5892	0.4610	0.463
Business and Consumer Magazines	6	5	-0.2240	-0.2119	0.0811	0.0767
Fashion Magazines	5	6	0.1336	0.14345	0.6144	0.6596
Cultural, Intellectual Magazines	7	–	–	–	–	–
Local News	3	4	0.3110	0.3121	-0.4279	-0.4293

they are (1) Homemaker Magazines, (2) National and International News, (3) Movie, Romance Magazines, (4) Local News, (5) Business and Consumer agazines, and (6) Fashion Magazines. The results generally support earlier findings when the factors and magazines were individually evaluated. The surprise inclusion among the top factors is Movie, Romance Magazines.

Although two discriminant functions were generated, the first function dominated the second completely (Table 34). It is eigenvalue had a relative percentage of 86.62 compared to 13.32 of the second function. The corresponding chi-square values were 58.6 (12.df) for the first function with a significance of 0.0 and 8.79 (5df) for the second function with a significance of 0.12. The group centroids on both functions, for the respective groups are shown in Figure 6.

The discriminant function is evaluated also for its predictive ability. Table 35 presents the number of hits and misses. Using the validating sample, the discriminant function correctly classified 52% of the traditionalists, 41% of the moderates and 67% of the feminists. More moderates were classified as traditionalists than feminists. This confirms the view that the reading habits of moderates tend to be more in line with the traditionalists than feminists. The probability than any individual would be classified into one of the groups is 0.33 or equal between the groups. Given this prior probability, the overall prediction is impressive.

To summarize the magazine readership characteristics of the groups revealed significant differences in the discriminant analysis. The differences point to confirm the basic fact that feminists appear to read magazines with intellectual and national and international news content. Traditionalists and moderates prefer to read more homemaker and local news magazines. The group centroids indicate that the general magazine readership profile of the

TABLE 34 DISCRIMINANT ANALYSIS

(Magazine Readership)

	Discriminant Function 1	Discriminant Function 2
Group Centroids:		
Traditionalists	0.3651	-0.2829
Moderates	0.3653	0.2828
Feminists	-0.7304	0.0001
Eigenvalue	0.3669	0.0567
Relative Percentage	86.62	13.38
Canonical Correlation	0.518	0.232
Wilks' Lambda	0.6923	0.9464
Chi-Square	58.649	8.794
Degrees of Freedom	12	5
Significance	0.0000	0.118

FIGURE 6. DISCRIMINANT ANALYSIS MAGAZINE READERSHIP VARIABLES

DISCRIMINANT SCORE 1 (HORIZONTAL) VS. DISCRIMINANT SCORE 2 (VERTICAL)

GROUP CENTROIDS T*(TRADITIONAL), M*(MODERATE), F*(FEMINIST).

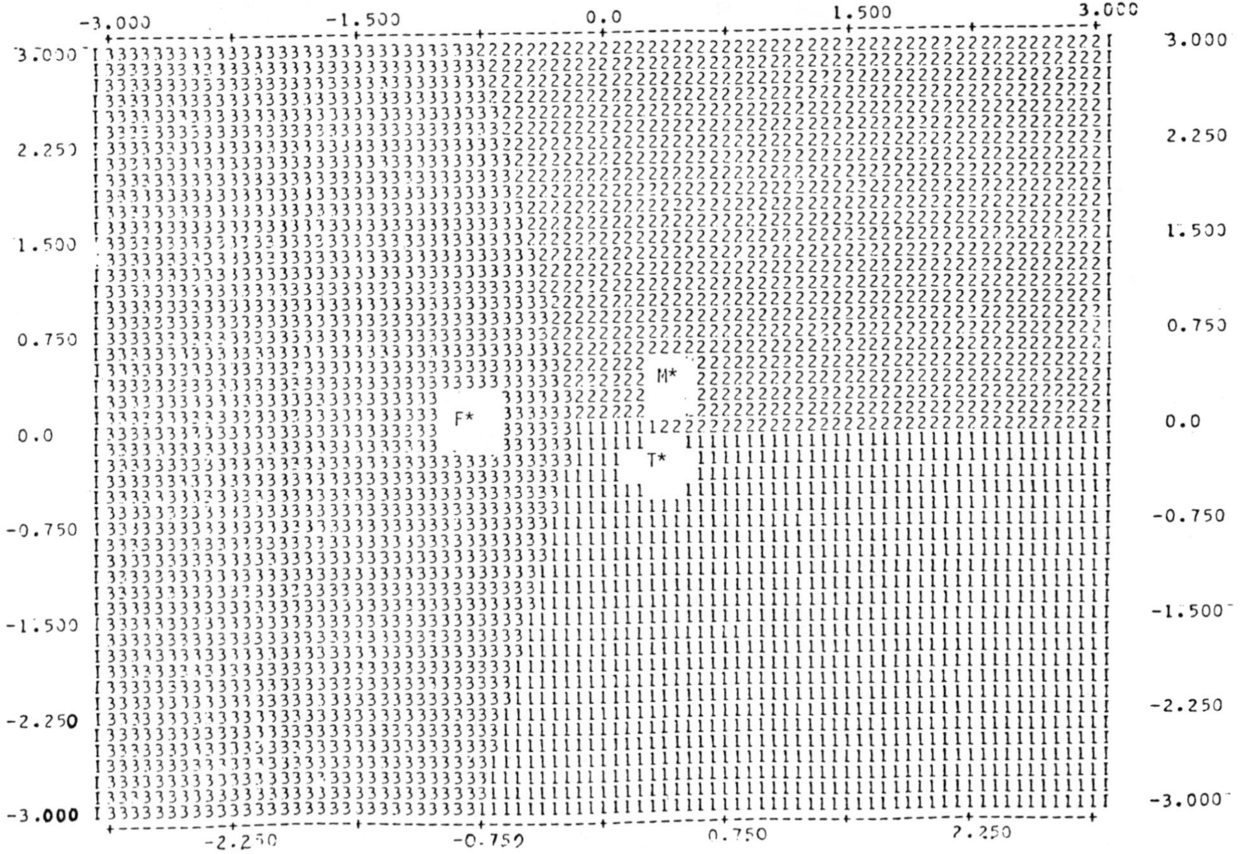

TABLE 35 DISCRIMINANT ANALYSIS
(Magazine Readership)

A. Prediction Results – With Original Sample

Actual Group	No. of Cases	Predicted Group Membership		
		Group 1	Group 2	Group 3
1. Traditionalists	55	29 (52.7%)	17 (30.9%)	9 (16.4%)
2. Moderates	55	20 (36.4%)	20 (36.4%)	15 (27.3%)
3. Feminists	55	9 (16.4%)	7 (12.7%)	39 (70.9%)

B. Prediction Results – With Validating Sample

Actual Group	No. of Cases	Predicted Group Membership		
		Group 1	Group 2	Group 3
1. Traditionalists	56	29 (51.8%)	17 (30.4%)	10 (17.9%)
2. Moderates	54	22 (40.7%)	22 (40.7%)	10 (18.5%)
3. Feminists	58	10 (17.2%)	9 (15.5%)	39 (17.2%)

traditionalists and moderates is similar and that of the feminists different
from both. This also came out in the classification of the validating sample.
The two factors which indicate small differences, if any, between the groups
were Business and Consumer Magazines and Fashion Magazines.

SUMMARY AND IMPLICATIONS

The major objective of the study was to evaluate the significance of
the women's movement to marketing. It sought to do so through an analysis of
sociological theories on changing roles of women and empirical investigations
involving the survey of female population between the ages of 18 and 45, living in the Syracuse urbanized area. Three groups of women were identified on
the basis of their scores on a Feminism scale and were labeled as Traditionalists, Moderates and Feminists.

In this concluding chapter, the following issues are discussed.

[1]   Summary of the results of the study

[2]   The major implications of the study for marketing

[3]   Limitations of the study and guidelines for future research

[1]   Summary of the Results

The study was operationalized by evaluating three groups of women labeled
as Traditionalists, Moderates and Feminists, on certain life style, demographic
and media dimensions. A mail survey was conducted in the Syracuse urbanized
area with the population consisting of all women between the ages of 18 and 45
and living within the designated area. A random sample of 333 women was selected
for a response rate of 41%, using a three stage stratified cluster sampling
procedure. The sample of women was classified into three groups on the basis
of the scores they received on Arnott's Feminism scale (1972). The sample consisted of 111 Traditionalists, 109 Moderates and 113 Feminists.

Various life style and demographic measures were included in the study and
group differences were examined using a variety of statistical techniques.
Specifically, four research questions were formulated at the outset of this

udy, and a multiphase research project* was designed to gather and analyze
ta for the examination of these questions. The major findings and conclu-
ons related to these questions are summarized below.

search Question 1 - Are the life style dimensions common to all the groups
     selected for the study?
e life style dimensions were selected based on three criteria (a) relevance
 Feminist movement, (b) relevance to marketing and (c) measurability.
e dimensions included attitudinal, personality and behavioral aspects of
fe style. Thus the following dimensions were hypothesized as representative
asures for the present research.

     Innovative Behavior -

     Opinion Leadership -

     Self-Confidence -

     Social Responsibility -

     Attitude Toward Television -

     Leisure Mindedness -

     Fashion and Personal Appearance -

     Role Portrayal of Women in Advertisements -

     Toys and Sex Symbolism -

     Life Simplification Products -

     Frozen Food Consumption -

 appropriate questionnaire was developed to gather data on the above dimen-
ons as well as demographic characteristics and magazine reading habits.

     In order to verify that the dimensions were common to all groups, separate
ctor Analyses were performed using individual group data on life style meas-
es. Factor analysis can be used to check the stability of factors or under-
A flowchart of the Methodology is presented in Figure 4. (p. 26)

lying dimensions across different sub-samples. The results showed that all but one life style dimension were extracted in each analysis. The dimension which failed to emerge was Social Responsibility and the over all result confirmed the hypothesis that the life style dimensions are common to all the groups.

Research Question 2 - Do the life style dimensions have the same significance to each group?

The purpose of this question was to verify that although the life style dimensions may be common to all the groups indicating their stability, each dimension and associated life style statements will have different significance to the respective groups. The earlier factor analysis on separate group data revealed that the order in which the factors were extracted was different for each group. Also the variable loadings on each factor were not the same.

The analysis relative to this question was carried out by first combining da for all groups and factoring the life style statements. Individual statements on each dimension were evaluated for the degree of agreement or disagreement they received from the three groups. The analysis revealed that the extracted dimensions matched all the hypothesized dimensions with the exception of "Social Responsibility". The dimensions in the order of their contribution to total variance were labeled:

> Sex Stereotyping
>
> Self-Confidence
>
> Fashion and Personal Appearance
>
> Television Viewing
>
> Life Simplification Products
>
> Leisure-work Attitude

Innovative Behavior

Active-Leisure Behavior

Opinion Leadership

Frozen Foods

An analysis of the individual life style statements revealed that the statements which differentiated the groups most were those grouped under two hypothesized dimensions "Women's Role Portrayal in Advertising" and "Toys and Sex Symbolism" with the Feminists and Traditionalists taking extreme positions on almost all the statements. Other items which showed some differences were grouped under "Attitude Toward Television Viewing" and "Leisure Activities". Moderate to low differences were found among statements associated with "Self-Confidence", "Fashion Behavior", "Life Simplification Products" and "Innovative Behavior". Practically no differences were found on statements pertaining to "Opinion Leadership", and "Frozen Foods".

A factor analysis was also performed using magazine readership data for all the groups combined. Thirty four magazines were selected representing different readership appeals. The analysis yielded following clusters of magazines (factors),in order of their contribution to the total variance:

Home Maker Magazines

Movie, Romance Magazines

National and International News

Business and Consumer Magazines

Fashion Magazines

Cultural, Intellectual Magazines

Local News

The two groups of magazines which accounted for the largest differences between the groups were 'Home Maker Magazines' and 'National and International News Magazines'. Moderates and Traditionalists tended to read more Home Maker Magazines while Feminists indicated a greater readership of the latter. All groups showed lowest readership values on 'Movie, Romance Magazines' and next to the lowest on 'Cultural Intellectual Magazines'.

In terms of individual magazines, those which revealed major readership differences between the groups were as follows:

(a) <u>High Traditionalists and Moderate Readership</u> and <u>Relatively Low Feminist Readership</u>:

Reader's Digest, Good Housekeeping, Family Circle, Woman's Day, Better Homes and Gardens

(b) <u>High Feminist Readership and Relatively Low to Moderate Traditionalist and Moderate Readership</u>:

Time, Newsweek, New York Times, Ms.

(c) <u>High to Moderate Readership in all Groups</u>:

Syracuse Local Newspapers, National Geographic Magazine, Cosmopolitan, Glamour.

(d) <u>Low Readership in all Groups</u>:

All remaining magazines.

<u>Research Question 3</u> - Do the groups represent different demographic characteristics?

It has been suggested by a few critics that the feminist movement was a middle-class intellectual affair. This remark by itself suggests that there ought to be differences between the groups based on demographic characteristics.

The purpose of the question was to verify if demographic variables did differentiate between the groups and if so, to what extent. The variables chosen for the study were (a) Age, (b) Education, (c) Family Income, (d) Religious Grouping, (e) Race, (f) Household Status, (g) Work Status and (h) Marital Status. The results are summarized as follows.

Highly significant differences were found between the groups based on Age, Education, Religion, Household Status and Work Status. No significant differences were found in the case of Marital Status, Race and Family Income. In general, feminists compared to the other groups, were found to be younger, better educated and revealed a greater sense of independence in terms of how they perceived themselves within the household. As far as the religious affiliation was concerned, more traditionalists were Roman Catholic and more feminists were Jewish with the moderates in the middle. However, each group had about the same proportion of Protestants. Generally, across all variables, moderates tended to cluster in the middle, with some characteristics similar to feminists and some others more similar to traditionalists.

In response to the observation that feminist movement could be considered middle-class intellectual affair, one could say that the results partially confirmed this. However, the changing environment and the spread of ideas would not hold this to be true very long.

Research Question 4 - Do the differences in the life style dimensions
    and demographic and magazine readership measures significantly
    discriminate between the groups?

The previous research questions indicated some apparent differences between the three groups. The exact nature of differences needed to be established with a more rigorous and powerful technique. This was done using stepwise multiple-discriminant analysis in two phases. In the first phase all the life style dimensions and demographic measures were combined to form the independent variables for the discriminant analysis. In the second phase the analysis was performed using magazine readership factors. While most of the differences were previously evaluated in a uni-variate basis, in the present scheme, one got to look at the group differences with the simultaneous presence of all variables or on a multivariate basis.

The first analysis was carried out using the factor scores on the life style dimensions and the direct measures on demographic variables. A total of 18 variables were entered in the analysis and 8 of them were found significant on their combined discriminating ability. In terms of the magnitude of the discriminating coefficients the variables were, (a) Sex Stereotyping, (b) Age, (c) Education, (d) Self-Confidence, (e) Marital Status, (f) Active-Leisure Behavior, (g) Fashion Behavior and (h) Life Simplification Products.

In earlier uni-variate analysis, the first three variables were found to be of highest significance. That this result is validated in the discriminant analysis is quite comforting. However, based on earlier findings, one did not expect to see Marital Status, Fashion Behavior and Life Simplification Products. While these were surprising inclusions, the surprising omissions were Work Status, Household Status, Religion and Innovative Behavior which were expected to be in the discriminant set.

The overall result confirms that life style and demographic variables were significant enough to discriminate between the three groups and supported the earlier finding about the three most important differentiating variables.

A second analysis was performed using magazine readership factors. Once again the input to the discriminant procedure were the factor scores obtained

from the factor analysis of magazine variables. Out of the seven variables
entered in the analysis, all but one were retained. In order of importance
(the magnitude of the discriminant coefficients) they were (a) Home Maker
Magazines, (b) National and International News, (c) Movie, Romance Magazines,
(d) Local News, (e) Business and Consumer Magazines and (f) Fashion Magazines. The excluded variable was "Cultural, Intellectual Magazines". This
was a surprising omission because of the inclusion of "Movie, Romance Magazines".

Over all, the results supported earlier findings that the two most important factors which revealed significant differences between the groups were
"Home Maker Magazines" and "National and International News".

[2] Marketing Implications Of The Study
The overall purpose of the study was to evaluate the significance of the
women's movement to marketing. As an important social force the movement has
made an impact onthe American scene arousing considerable interest among social
scientists in general and marketers in particular. To the marketer, the significance of the feminist movement lies in the potential influence it has over
the attitudes, opinions and behavior of women in the market place. The marketing implications of this study are developed by integrating the results of
the study with observations that have already stood the test of empirical validation and with conjectures which have some sound basis. A scenario of changes
with implications to marketing is shown in Table 36.
Sex Stereotyping:
The most important dimension to emerge from this study is Sex Stereotyping
which includes two hypothesized dimensions - Role Portrayal of women in advertisements and Toys and Sex Symbolism. Together they represent an issue that is

TABLE 36 A SUMMARY OF MARKETING OPPORTUNITIES AS A RESULT OF CHANGING SOCIAL ROLES

Existing Emphasis	Changing to
Family	
Woman as the family purchasing agent	Man and woman both family purchasing agents Man in the role of domesticated parent (Concern for child's needs etc.,)
Career and Jobs	
Women work for increasing family income	Women work for self-expression, independence and enhancing family status. Men compromise career ambitions and choose professions that give personal satisfaction.
Advertising Images	
Women portrayed in traditional roles mother-wife-maid, etc.	Possible new roles for women, e.g., doctors, scientists, lawyers and other professionals - In general bread-winner roles (Since many women will still be involved in housework, they may develop a loss of prestige in the housework role. Marketers should be sensitive to this issue.)
Image of woman in advertisements as nurturant, passive, compliant	Image of women in advertisements as aggressive, professionally minded and creative Creating new image of men as a result of changing social realities
Leisure Activities and Social Life	
Women not engaging in physically demanding activities Participation in home centered leisure activities with major emphasis on recreation.	Women engaging in physically demanding activities Participation in self-expressive leisure activities
Social activities (partying, clubs, etc.) for status enhancement	Social activities secondary to higher pursuits.
Products and Services	
Targets for conventional feminine and family-oriented products	Targets also for non-conventional products, non-sexist products and new status symbols
Purchase of labor saving products to be able to give more time to family care	Purchase of labor saving products so that leisure time can be used for personal pleasure, other life objectives.
Product-oriented asset ownership	Time-oriented use values

close to the heart of the feminists. The views of the traditionalists are more sympathetic to the role portrayals and Sex Stereotyping in general.

The roles portrayed by women in magazine advertisements have been studied recently by several authors (Courtney and Lockeretz, 1971; Wagner and Banos, 1973; Sexton and Haberman 1974; Venkatesan and Losco, 1975; Belkaoui, 1976). Courtney and Lockeretz studied the stereotyped images of women in seven popular magazines printed in 1970 and pointed out the great disparity between the roles portrayed by women and the true range of women's roles in American society. In a follow up study, Wagner and Banos found increases in the proportion of female workers shown in professional and other white-collar occupations. In a very comprehensive study of magazine advertisement reported by Venkatesan and Losco, three phases were examined, (a) (1959-1963), the pre-women's movement period; (b) 1964-68, the early stages of women's movement and (c) 1969-1971, the period of impact. They classified magazines into general, women's, and men's. Their main findings are as follows:

During the 13 year period three roles which emerged most frequently were (a) women as sexual objects, (b) woman as physically beautiful, and (c) woman as dependent on man. Women were portrayed as housewives more often in 1959-1963 than during other two periods. Women were portrayed more often as being concerned with physically beauty during 1964-71 than any other period. The data also indicate that the portrayal of women as sex objects decreased from 1959 to 1971. However, the authors conclude, the change of role portrayals at the end of 1971 have been minimal.

The implications to the marketers are that women's role portrayals in advertising should truly represent the changes occurring in reality. At the same time, the advertisers must selectively respond to the environment because there is still a large body of women who have not been swept by these changes but do in fact hold on to traditional roles and associated values.

Another dimension of Sex Stereotyping is Toys and Sex Symbolism. The reason why toys were selected was because they represent a fundamental idea in sex role definition at a very early age in human socialization. According to Pogrebin (1973),

> "Studies have shown that, by the age of three, children show a distinct preference for sex-typed activities which reflect what they have absorbed from the culture ......Toys and games make a vital contribution to a growing character, personality, and temperament...... Toys have been known to inspire occupational choice, unleash artistic talent or leave an emotional imprint on life...."

To the feminists, toys are a strong symbol of stereotyping which inhibits the aspirations of women and imposes restrictions on their potential development. In the present study, overwhelming differences were found between feminists and traditionalists (with moderates taking the middle ground) in their perceptions of what might be the kind of toys that boys and girls should plat with.

To the marketers, the implications are in understanding the aspirations of the various segments and providing products and services that match those aspirations. To the extent that women are fighting against stereotype manifestations in product offerings, they are seeking a change representing an image of rationality, functional appeal and purposeful identity. This means that marketers should try to desex product offerings wherever possible.

Household Purchasing Decisions

In marketing, much research has been done on "purchasing decisions" within the context of family (Davis, 1976). Generally, the husband was considered as the head of household but the wife was regarded as the family purchasing agent

for a variety of products, and indeed, most advertisements for everyday consumer products are still addressed to the 'wife (mother)' in the family.
By the same token, as the head of the household, the male was a logical target
for products which required major investment decisions.

In the domesticated role of the housewife, a woman's purchasing decisions
are governed by the occupation and income of the husband, the residential lo-
cation of the family, the social network of housewives in the neighborhood
and the presence of children and the demands on child care. With more women
going into professions and their growing career commitment, the amount of time
women spend with children is changing along with their attitudes toward child
care. The dependence on male household head is also diminishing. In the
present study, about the same proportion (70%) in each group indicated that
they were married (Table 9). However, 28% of the traditionalists designated
themselves as 'housewives' while only 16% of the moderates and 8% of the feminists did so. Similarly, 84% of the feminists called themselves 'cohead of
household' compared with 61% in the case of moderates and 51% in the case of
traditionalists (Table 16). One reason for this could be that more feminists
are working compared to the members of the other two groups. The data on
'work status' (Table 14) shows that (a) 34% of the traditionalists are full-
time employed compared to 48% of the moderates and 40% of the feminists and
(b) 34% of the traditionalists said that they were 'keeping house' while 16%
of the moderates and 14% of the feminists did so. However, the differences
in work status do not explain the magnitude of the differences in the perceptions of the respondents about their household status. These self-
perceptions are extremely significant to the marketer because of the shifts
they suggest in attitudinal variables and decision making roles within the
context of the family. In practical terms, this would mean that there is at

least a significant group of women who do not feel obliged to buy products or make other consumption decisions to enhance their image as a "housewife". The classic story of the instant coffee not selling because it would give an image of "lazy housewife" may not be so significant in today's changing environment. To the changing woman, a status car, the deed to her house, her job title and her executive suite may be as important.

Changing Roles of Men

With the gradual crumbling of "the husband-breadwinner" and "wife-homemaker" model, the traditional focus of the marketer may undergo a change to include men (Crittenden, 1977). The conventional masculine image in advertising is that of a success oriented, self-confident, logically thinking and professionally strong individual. While nobody would argue that this impression will give place entirely to one of sensual, warm, conforting mother-like image, some changes need to be considered. Men's roles vis-a-vis the family and children are subject to some shifts, creating a new sense of values and life styles (Weigand, 1973; Ackerman, 1973). Firstly, in raising children, the shifting roles of fathers is indicated by Weigand (1973). "As women discover that fulfillment in their lives can be more than raising children and ministering to a husband, and as men come to know that there is more to parenthood than bringing home a weekly pay check, men taking an active, even dominant role in the rearing of children will become increasingly common. Also, with increasing number of divorces the role of the single father becomes a fairly common reality."

A second aspect of man's changing roles arises as a result of wife pursuing a career. With the careers of wives becoming fairly adequate for family status and its economic strength, men are likely to choose low paying but interesting jobs (Farrell, 1974, ch. 10; Crittenden, 1976). These jobs might release men from existing competitive pressures of the work environment allow-

ing them to devote greater time among other things to satisfying family needs
in new roles. For the present, however, the situation has been that if the
wife wished to pursue a career and "the husband's time must be spent caring
for children, the decision is usually made not to have children." (Mary
Rowe, as quoted in Farrell, 1974). Assuming that in the future the domesticated male, not necessarily in the familiar image of domesticated female, is
a likely possibility the marketer may have to contend with two family purchasing agents sharing a similar concern for family needs. Accordingly, appropriate
products and services and new communication appeals would have to be developed
in response to the changing value systems of men.

Fashion Products and Personal Appearance

The study has shown that all groups of women are equally interested in
shopping for clothes' in "feeling attractive' and in 'thumbing through fashion
magazines'. This does not necessarily suggest that they reveal identical
preferences for any given product or for any particular mode of dressing. It
is more than likely that their specific behavior patterns, tastes and preferences
are different. The institutionalized attitudes towards female fashion and personal appearance have come under much criticism. It has been argued by some
feminists that the infinite variety of cosmetic and socially conspicuous products adorning female bodies are a deliberate male invention, arbitrarily designed and culturally imposed (Ramsey 1972, Schoolman 1973 and Altman 1973).
Apparently, there is a growing consciousness in dress habits that seeks a greater
sense of freedom.

With the rise in discretionary income among women, there is every reason
to believe that more consumer dollars will be spent on female fashion and cosmetic products. The exact nature of these expenditures is what interests most

marketers. The traditional view about women is that they dressed to please men or in a display of conspicuous consumption and less for what the clothes meant in terms of practical utility and comfort (Carden, 1974). Obviously such a restricted view of the feminine motivation should be revised by marketers to include changing values of women who are joining the work force in greater numbers. These women will probably be less concerned with fears of social rejection and would buy various products with a greater degree of deliberateness and less adherence to prescribed norms. The implications to the marketers are in terms of effective product positioning and in understanding the evaluative behavior of female purchases.

Magazine Reading Habits

The analysis brought out clearly some differences between the groups in their magazine reading habits. To the advertiser of products the implications are in terms of reaching the right audience through a particular media vehicle.

It is obvious from the results that Reader's Digest cannot be used effectively to reach feminists in particular and younger audience in general while it certainly appeals to traditionalists and moderates. Similarly the editorial profile Ms. magazine does not favor advertising for products with traditional appeal because its readers are mostly feminists. The two magazines represent two extremes in their philosophies with various other magazines lying somewhere in between the two.

Fashion magazines represent roughly equal readership among groups. This poses a challenge to advertisers who use the same media vehicle to appeal to different segments with different tastes and preferences.

Feminists constitute a major readership group for national and international news magazines with the two other groups occupying relatively lower readership positions. In allocation of advertising funds, marketers can use this information for effective segmentation.

Homemaker magazines are mostly read by moderates and traditionalists. Their present appeals are not effectively directed against feminists. Since feminists are also involved in homemaking activities, these magazines should try to change their appeals without giving up their present audience or else, new magazines may enter the publishing world to cater to feminists.

Moderates and feminists more than the traditionalists, appear to read consumer related magazines. The implications are that the members of these two groups use independent information search whereas the traditionalists either believe the business claims of the product or are unable to make independent information searches of their own.

Local newspapers are popular among all groups. This is inevitable because the local newspapers serve different needs not met by other publications.

Cultural and intellectual magazines do not seem to command significant readership from any group. The very low readership suggests that these magazines are predominantly read by men. The advertisers may want to explore the reasons further to evaluate their usefulness as efficient media vehicles.

Leisure Activities and Social Life

The study has revealed some moderate differences between the groups in their attitudes toward leisure and work. One of the interesting outcomes of the study is that more feminists claimed to be engaging in sports activities in their free time and almost every feminist was heartened to see "women participate in outdoor sports". The proportion of traditionalists and moderates who answered positively to these issues is also very high but lower than feminists. This suggests that there is a general awareness about outdoor sports which till recently was the province of men. It would seem as though sports activities would be the first to establish parity between men and women, among the various areas where such parity is being sought.

In recent years women have been found to involve more and more in physically demanding activities. According to Shaffer (1972) a medical scientist, "the evidence seems clear that from a constitutional point of view, woman is the stronger sex". Another writer claims "the male's 'overwhelming' superiority of strength and endurance may be more an artifact of social or cultural restriction imposed on the female.....than a result of true biological differences in performance potential between the sexes". (Harris, 1972). Both statements have been made in the context of sports but do have implications to other leisure pursuits which create many opportunities for marketers to develop appropriate products and services. (Hemmerdinger, 1972).

If one assumes that women's participation in sports activities would equal men's, it is also likely that the basic motivations for such participation would change. In fact, in the past, women engaging in various social activities did so to 'kill time' or for status enhancement. With social and personal priorities changing because of greater labor force participation of women, social activities may become secondary to higher pursuits in life. Participation in leisure activities would be to enhance self-expression and to satisfy personal needs and with a view to making the best use of time. It has been pointed out by some social scientists that many women with full time jobs and careers do, in deference to established social attitudes, end up doing the same amoung of housework during their non-office hours thus finding very little time to social and leisure pursuits of any kind. The marketers would do well to understand the needs of such women more closely.

Products and Services

Marketers have already, successfully, marketed many products with modifications in design or packaging or advertising appeals. Many of the products so modified exist within the context of conventional social roles and can be described as basically, responses to 'trendy' directions. The changing women's roles suggest a future emphasis on non-conventional products, non-sexist products and products that represent new status symbols. There may be a shift from product-oriented asset ownership to time-oriented use values. Marketers will be facing more and more discerning buyers among women, less subject to traditional psychological symbolism in product appeals. Their needs will be articulated more in terms of their careers, professions and other new goals.

[3] Limitations of the Study and Suggestions for Future Research

Study Limitations

No study, however well conceived and intended, can accomplish everything it set out to do. Nor can it foresee all the possibilities that only a hindsight can visualize. The present research attempted to examine the changing roles of women and their implications to marketing. It was exploratory in scope paving way for some more exhaustive studies in the future.

Within the resources available a probability sampling design was implemented, but some of the problems of the mail survey were encountered. In particular, the low response rate (41%) could have been improved if respondents were contacted personally rather than via the mail. However, as mail survey responses go the present rate of response was impressive.

The overall sampling design could have been improved with better preparation of lists of female population but the cost would be too prohibitive.
Therefore, the sampling was carried out based on the assumption that very
few households will have more than one female in the age group 18-45. Of
course, this assumption was not without sufficient foundation. Hindsight
suggests that the bias due to this assumption could have been estimated by
merely inserting a question in the questionnaire asking the respondent to indicate the member of females in the same household between the ages of 18
and 45.

Regarding the internal validity and external validity* of the research,
some comments are in order. Much care was taken in preparation of the questionnaire, selection of life style dimensions and in the use of statistical procedures. Internal validity could have been improved by using non-parametric
discriminant analysis, a procedure rarely used in social sciences but available in statistical theory. Some of the biases in mail survey could have
affected internal validity. The question of external validity raises some
problems. How generalizable are the results? If the sample can be considered
representative of Syracuse population, the results can be generalized to that
population. Extending this question further, one may ask whether the results
can be generalized to a larger population, say all American females between
the ages 18 and 45. This really depends on how representative is Syracuse of
the overall population of the country. While one cannot answer the question
of external validity with in definite terms, it can be argued that in this

---

* Validity is defined as the degree to which the researcher has measured what
  he set out to measure. Internal validity refers to the question of whether
  the results would have been different if different methods had been used.
  External validity refers to the question of generalizability of the results
  to larger population.

study an attempt was made to construct a sample design based on probability concepts and a reasonably representative sample was obtained within the constraints of this research.

Suggestions for Future Research

The study was not meant as a comprehensive analysis of the changing roles of women and their economic and marketing significance. It attempted to examine some propositions not tested in marketing literature, relative to attitudes, opinions and interests of three segments of women identified on a feminism scale. The following suggestions are made for future research.

1. A more systematic sampling scheme should be developed to represent the national population.

2. Replication of the study should be done with similar or different populations to test the consistency of the results. For example, the attitudes of non-white population need to be examined for comparability.

3. One of the assumptions of the study was the existence of three groups based on a feminism scale. A determination should be made if there are more or fewer groups of women based on a natural clustering scheme.

4. The study was limited to non-product-specific dimensions. Researchers may be interested in extending the study to include product-specific dimensions.

5. Some of the results pertaining to possible advertising and product strategies are of a general nature. It may be necessary to evaluate specific advertising appeals and product concepts in a more rigorous experimental research.

6. One of the developments in the changing female environment is their career development and commitment. Since family consumption behavior is an important topic for marketers, the implications of female careers should be evaluated in terms of dual career family needs and goals.

7. It was suggested in the study that the changing life styles of women are bound to have effect on the life styles of men. A follow up study involving men would be very logical in this context.

8. Another area for further study is the examination of attitudes toward various television programs. In the present study magazine readership profiles were developed. A similar evaluation can be undertaken to include other media.

9. Because of the nature of some of the data in the study, it may be necessary to use non-parametric procedures for increasing the validity of the results.

Conclusions

The marketing implications of changing women's roles have been discussed in the hope that they will provide a basis for developing appropriate product and communication strategies. These strategies will be responses to impending changes in the environment.

In responding to the changes, however, a note of caution has to be made. One can do no better than quoting Miller and Marguilies (1974) who have reacted to some marketing responses to changing life styles of women.

> "...this suggests that women are creating a 'life style'
> --perhaps a style of liberation, an image created by
> their clothes, their far out new interests, their rhetoric.
> Many of the media are picking up on the life style of
> liberation because 'style' is what they are selling.
> However, women who are changing their perceptions of
> themselves and their realities are not just living a
> 'life style,' they are living and changing their actual
> 'lives.' It is just a put down to call this a 'style'
> ...if 'liberation' gets sold to women by the media as
> cosmetics, clothes, style, or image, they obscure the
> real demands women are making and perpetuate the very
> social and political structure we are trying to change.
> This can slow down our progress, and we should not
> let it happen."

APPENDIX 1

(Life Style and Demographic Questionnaire)

Contents

a) Cover letter for Mail Survey.

b) Follow-up Card.

c) Letter to Non-respondents

d) Questionnaire.

MANAGEMENT RESEARCH CENTER | SCHOOL OF MANAGEMENT

129 COLLEGE PLACE | SYRACUSE, NEW YORK 13210
PHONE 315 423-2052

April, 16, 1976

Dear Friend:

With various kinds of mail coming into your home every day, it must be really difficult for you to pay attention to every letter. We hope, however, that you can give a few minutes of your time for a valid educational purpose.

The School of Management Research Center is engaged in an opinion survey of women in the 18-45 age group. We need your assistance to make this research possible. If you are a female between 18 and 45, please help us by answering the enclosed questionnaire. If you are not, will you please give the questionnaire to a member of your household who is a female between 18 and 45.

We wish to emphasize that this research is a legitimate one and any individual response will be held in strictest confidence. No individual's name is sought nor will it be revealed. The information used in our study will only be used in an aggregate form.

The purpose of the study is to survey the attitudes and opinions of women about various current topics that are likely to be important to social scientists and public and business organizations.

Thank you for your assistance. Please used the stamped envelope to return the questionnaire.

Sincerely,

David L. Wilemon, Director
Management Research Center

DLW:cm
Enclosures

Alladi Venkatesh
Principal Investigator

(Cover letter for Mail Survey)

Management Research Center
Syracuse University

Dear Friend:

Recently, we sent you a questionnaire requesting
your participation in our study. If you haven't
returned it with your responses, would you please take
a few minutes to fill in the questionnaire and return
it to us in the envelope sent earlier. If your response
is already mailed please ignore this request. Thank
you for your participation.

Sincerely,

April 26,1976   David L. Wilemon
                                        Director

(Follow-up Card)

June 18, 1976

Dear Friend:

Some time ago we sent you a letter and a questionnaire, a copy of which is enclosed. We realize that you have very important matters to attend to and were unable to find the time to fill in the questionnaire. We are making this special request to you to give us a few minutes of your time.

By participating in our study, you would provide valuable assistance to us. As a token of our appreciation and gratitude for this assistance, we will send you a Bi-Centennial silver dollar. Just call Carolyn Miller at 423-2961 or 423-2962 or give us your name and address when returning the questionnaire, and we will send you the silver dollar promptly. Won't you please help us by returning the completed questionnaire in the stamped return envelope.

Incidentally, the questionnaire has to be filled out by a female between the ages of 18 and 45.

Thank you.

Sincerely,

Professor David L. Wilemon
School of Management

Alladi Venkatesh
Principal Investigator

DLW:pvs
Enclosures

(Letter to Non-respondents)

CHANGING DIMENSIONS IN THE LIFE STYLES OF WOMEN

MANAGEMENT   RESEARCH   CENTER
SCHOOL OF MANAGEMENT
SYRACUSE   UNIVERSITY
SYRACUSE, N.Y. 13210

(Questionnaire)

INSTRUCTIONS: In this part of the questionnaire you will find a number of statements. Please read each statement carefully. After each statement, there are five numbers, 1 to 5. The higher the number, the more you tend to agree with the statement. The lower the number, the more you tend to disagree with the statement. In particular, the numbers 1 to 5 may be described as follows:

> 1 means you definitely disagree with the statement.
> 2 means you moderately disagree with the statement.
> 3 means you neither agree nor disagree with the statement.
> 4 means you moderately agree with the statement.
> 5 means you definitely agree with the statement.

For each statement, circle the number that best describes your feelings about that statement. There are no best answers. The purpose of this survey will be best achieved if you describe yourself and state your opinions as accurately as possible. You may think many items are similar. Actually, no two items are exactly alike.

BE SURE TO CIRCLE AN ANSWER FOR EVERY ITEM

	Definitely Disagree				Definitely Agree
A woman should expect just as much freedom of action as a man	1	2	3	4	5
I often try new ideas before my friends do	1	2	3	4	5
Leisure activities express one's talents better than does a person's job	1	2	3	4	5
I couldn't get along without frozen foods	1	2	3	4	5
My friends or neighbors often come to me for advice	1	2	3	4	5
I feel capable of handling myself in most social situations	1	2	3	4	5
Television has added a great deal of enjoyment to my life	1	2	3	4	5
American advertisements picture a woman's place to be in the home	1	2	3	4	5
It is no use worrying about current events or public affairs; I can't do anything about them anyway	1	2	3	4	5
An important part of my life and activities is dressing smartly	1	2	3	4	5
I would like to see more and more young girls play with mechanical toys	1	2	3	4	5
The initiative in courtship should come from men	1	2	3	4	5
When I see a new brand of product on the shelf, I often buy it, just to see what it is like	1	2	3	4	5
I feel I am a member of more organizations than most women are	1	2	3	4	5
Leisure activities are more satisfying than a job	1	2	3	4	5
I consider it essential for most American families to own an automatic coffee maker	1	2	3	4	5
I sometimes influence what my friends buy	1	2	3	4	5
I seldom fear my actions will cause others to have a low opinion of me	1	2	3	4	5
I don't like watching television and so I rarely do	1	2	3	4	5
American advertisements seem to have recognized the changes in women's roles	1	2	3	4	5
Every person should give some of their time for the good of the country	1	2	3	4	5
I love to shop for clothes	1	2	3	4	5
I would like to see boys playing with dolls just the way girls do	1	2	3	4	.5
The word obey should be removed from the marriage ceremony	1	2	3	4	5
Sometimes I buy things impulsively and do not feel sorry about it later	1	2	3	4	5
I feel I can talk to most of the people in the neighborhood any time I feel like it	1	2	3	4	5
Ambitions are more realized on the job than in one's free time	1	2	3	4	5
I consider it essential for most American families to own a dishwasher	1	2	3	4	5
I indulge in sports activities in my free time	1	2	3	4	5

	Definitely Disagree				Definitely Agree

It is encouraging to see women participate in outdoor sports as men do. . . 1 2 3 4 5

It doesn't bother me to have to enter a room where other people have gathered already and are talking 1 2 3 4 5

In group discussions, I usually feel my opinions are inferior 1 2 3 4 5

The decision whether to seek an abortion should rest with the wife . . . .

I watch television to be entertained 1 2 3 4 5

American advertisements depict women as sexual objects 1 2 3 4 5

Our country would be better off if we didn't have so many elections and people didn't have to vote so often 1 2 3 4 5

At school I volunteered for special projects 1 2 3 4 5

I like to feel attractive 1 2 3 4 5

Her sex should not disqualify a woman from any occupation 1 2 3 4 5

I watch television more than I should 1 2 3 4 5

I don't make a favorable first impression on people 1 2 3 4 5

I would feel extremely uncomfortable if I accidentally went to a formal party in ordinary clothes 1 2 3 4 5

The husband should be regarded as the legal representative of the family in matters of law 1 2 3 4 5

During leisure time I like to relax by reading a book or listening to music 1 2 3 4 5

I consider it essential for most American families to own a food disposal unit 1 2 3 4 5

When confronted by a group of strangers, my first reaction is one of shyness and inferiority 1 2 3 4 5

I would like to go to the beauty parlor as often as I can 1 2. 3 4 5

Motherhood is the "ideal" career for most women 1 2 3 4 5

I don't spend much time worrying about what people think of me 1 2 3 4 5

I don't pay much attention to television commercials 1 2 3 4 5

American advertisements depict women as independent without needing the protection of men 1 2 3 4 5

I am rarely at a loss for words when I am introduced to someone 1 2 3 4 5

Women should subordinate their career to home duties to a greater extent than men 1 2 3 4 5

People come to me more often than I go to them for information about brands 1 2 3 4 5

Boys and girls should play with the same kind of toys 1 2 3 4 5

Within marriage a woman should be free to withhold or initiate sex intimacy as she chooses 1 2 3 4 5

I enjoy looking through fashion magazines to see what is new in fashions. . 1 2 3 4 5

I depend on frozen food for at least one meal a day 1 2 3 4 5

Girls should be trained to be homemakers and boys for an occupation suited to their talents 1 2 3 4 5

I like people who take risks in life without fear of what may happen . . . 1 2 3 4 5

If I am not working, I feel bored 1 2 3 4 5

I consider it essential for most American families to own a washer and drier 1 2 3 4 5

I like to do a lot of partying 1 2 3 4 5

Be Sure To Read These Instructions Before Starting On This Page

INSTRUCTIONS: Indicate by writing an "X" in each column how often you, personally, read each of the follo⟨w⟩
magazines and newspapers. By read, we mean that you spend at least 10 minutes with a newsp⟨aper⟩
and 20 minutes with a magazine. Each newspaper or magazine should have only one "X" after ⟨it⟩

	I Never Read It	I Occasionally Read It	I Read About Half the Issues	I Read About Two of Every Three Issues	I Read Almost Every Issue
Post Standard	[ ]	[ ]	[ ]	[ ]	[ ]
Herald Journal	[ ]	[ ]	[ ]	[ ]	[ ]
New York Times (Daily)	[ ]	[ ]	[ ]	[ ]	[ ]
New York Times (Sunday)	[ ]	[ ]	[ ]	[ ]	[ ]
Atlantic Monthly	[ ]	[ ]	[ ]	[ ]	[ ]
Better Homes and Gardens	[ ]	[ ]	[ ]	[ ]	[ ]
Business Week	[ ]	[ ]	[ ]	[ ]	[ ]
Consumer Bulletin	[ ]	[ ]	[ ]	[ ]	[ ]
Consumer Reports	[ ]	[ ]	[ ]	[ ]	[ ]
Cosmopolitan	[ ]	[ ]	[ ]	[ ]	[ ]
Esquire	[ ]	[ ]	[ ]	[ ]	[ ]
Family Circle	[ ]	[ ]	[ ]	[ ]	[ ]
Field and Stream	[ ]	[ ]	[ ]	[ ]	[ ]
Glamour	[ ]	[ ]	[ ]	[ ]	[ ]
Good Housekeeping	[ ]	[ ]	[ ]	[ ]	[ ]
Harper's	[ ]	[ ]	[ ]	[ ]	[ ]
Holiday	[ ]	[ ]	[ ]	[ ]	[ ]
House Beautiful	[ ]	[ ]	[ ]	[ ]	[ ]
Modern Romance	[ ]	[ ]	[ ]	[ ]	[ ]
Modern Screen	[ ]	[ ]	[ ]	[ ]	[ ]
Ms	[ ]	[ ]	[ ]	[ ]	[ ]
National Geographic	[ ]	[ ]	[ ]	[ ]	[ ]
Newsweek	[ ]	[ ]	[ ]	[ ]	[ ]
McCalls	[ ]	[ ]	[ ]	[ ]	[ ]
New Yorker	[ ]	[ ]	[ ]	[ ]	[ ]
Reader's Digest	[ ]	[ ]	[ ]	[ ]	[ ]
Saturday Review	[ ]	[ ]	[ ]	[ ]	[ ]
Sports Illustrated	[ ]	[ ]	[ ]	[ ]	[ ]
True Story	[ ]	[ ]	[ ]	[ ]	[ ]
True Confessions	[ ]	[ ]	[ ]	[ ]	[ ]
Time	[ ]	[ ]	[ ]	[ ]	[ ]
T.V. Guide	[ ]	[ ]	[ ]	[ ]	[ ]
U.S. News and World Report	[ ]	[ ]	[ ]	[ ]	[ ]
Woman's Day	[ ]	[ ]	[ ]	[ ]	[ ]
Other (specify)					
_____	[ ]	[ ]	[ ]	[ ]	[ ]
_____	[ ]	[ ]	[ ]	[ ]	[ ]
_____	[ ]	[ ]	[ ]	[ ]	[ ]

<u>Be Sure To Read These Instructions Before Starting On This Page</u>

STRUCTIONS: These questions ask for information about your present family/personal situation. Please answer the questions as completely as possible. When a line is provided, please write in your answer. Where a box is provided, please use an "X" to indicate this is the category which answers the question. Most questions have a box for answering.

What is your marital status?

[ ] Married   [ ] Widowed   [ ] Divorced   [ ] Separated   [ ] Never Married

What is the total number of children 16 years of age and under presently living in your home? _____

Please check which most appropriately describes your work status:

[ ] Working full-time   [ ] Working part-time   [ ] Unemployed, laid off, looking for work

[ ] Retired   [ ] With a job but temporarily out of work because of illness, strike

[ ] In school   [ ] Keeping house   [ ] Other (specify) _____

Do you own or rent the apartment or house you are currently living in? [ ] Rent   [ ] Own

Please check which most appropriately describes your household status:

[ ] Head of household   [ ] Housewife   [ ] Dependent   [ ] Co-head of household

Please indicate your religious denomination:

[ ] Protestant   [ ] Roman Catholic   [ ] Jewish   [ ] Other

Please check your race: [ ] White   [ ] Black   [ ] Spanish   [ ] Asian   [ ] Other

Please check your age group: [ ] 18-24   [ ] 25-30   [ ] 31-34   [ ] 35-39   [ ] 40-45

Please check the highest grade or school or college education you have completed:

[ ] Primary or elementary education   [ ] Some high school   [ ] High school graduate

[ ] Some college   [ ] College graduate   [ ] Post graduate

Please check into which of these income groups does your <u>total family</u> income fall:

[ ]   0 - $ 4,999   [ ] $ 5,000 - $ 9,999   [ ] $10,000 - $14,999   [ ] $15,000 - $19,999

[ ] $20,000 - $24,999   [ ] $25,000 - $29,999   [ ] $30,000 - $49,999   [ ] $50,000 and above

APPENDIX 2

(Self Designating Feminism Score Questionnaire)
and
(Arnott's Feminism Scale)

Graduate School of Management – Syracuse University

Dear Respondent,

The Graduate School of Management, Syracuse University, invites you to participate in a study concerning values and opinions of women in America. For the pilot study now in progress, we seek your assistance in answering the following questionnaire which should not take more than 5/10 minutes. Please answer all the questions because even if one question is left out the questionnaire becomes invalid. We do not require any personal information and any answer we receive will be used in an aggregate form only. Thank you for your time.

Questionnaire

PART I

1. Have you heard of Women's Liberation Movement or Feminist Movement?   Yes 1   No 2

2. Could you please tell us about your support for some of the issues that feminists are fighting for, listing below what those issues are? (Check appropriate box)

	Full Support	Partial	No Support
Issue 1 _____	[2]	[1]	[0]
Issue 2 _____	[2]	[1]	[0]
Issue 3 _____	[2]	[1]	[0]
Issue 4 _____	[2]	[1]	[0]

3. On a scale of 1 to 6 where 1 represents highly traditional woman and 6 represents high degree of feminism where would you place yourself? Circle the Number which most applied to you.

Extremely Traditional	Traditional	Middle of the Road but more Traditional	Middle of the Road but more Feministic	Feministic	Extremely Feministic
1	2	3	4	5	6

4. Can you recall reading any magazines which are primarily devoted to women's political and social issues in the past two years?   Yes 1   No 0

5. Would you please cite the names of those magazines?   1 1   2 2

6. We hear a lot of talk these days about liberals and conservatives. On a scale of 1 to 6 where would you place yourself? (1 represents extremely conservative and 6 represents extremely liberal). Circle appropriate number which best describes you.

Extremely Conservative	Conservative	Slightly Conservative	Slightly Liberal	Liberal	Extremely Liberal
1	2	3	4	5	6

PART II

In this part of the questionnaire there are ten statements. After each statement, there are numbers 1 to 5. The higher the number, the more you tend to agree with the statement. The lower the number, the more you tend to disagree. In particular, the numbers mean:

1 means you definitely disagree
2 means you moderately disagree
3 means you neither agree nor disagree
4 means you moderately agree
5 means you definitely agree

(PLEASE BE SURE TO CIRCLE AN ANSWER FOR EVERY ITEM)

	Definitely Disagree				Definitely Agree
A woman should expect as much freedom of action as man	1	2	3	4	5

The initiative in courtship should come from men

The word obey should be removed from marriage ceremony

The decision whether to seek an abortion should rest with the wife

Her sex should not disqualify a woman from any occupation

The husband should be regarded as the legal representative of the family in matters of law

Motherhood is ideal career for most women

Women should subordinate their career to home duties to a greater extent than men

Within marriage a woman should feel free to withhold or initiate sex as she chooses

Girls should be trained to be homemakers and boys for an occupation suited to their talents

APPENDIX 3

FACTOR ANALYSIS

A factor is a linear combination of the variables which have been measured. The factor by itself cannot be measured. In Factor Analysis, one can either describe a variable as linear combination of factors or a factor as a linear combination of variables. In the first case:

$$Z_{ji} = a_{j1} F_{i1} + a_{j2} F_{i2} + \ldots + a_{jm} F_{im}$$

where

i	refers to the individual ($i = 1 \ldots n$)
m	refers to the Factor F ($m = 1 \ldots p$)
j	refers to the variable x ($j = 1 \ldots k$)
a_{jm}	is the Factor Loading or the correlation between variable j and Factor m.
F_{im}	is the individual i's Factor Score (Factor Score is the computed measure on the Factor which cannot be directly measured)
Z_{ji}	is the standardized score of each individual i or variable j.

In the second case, we have:

$$F_i = \Sigma_j \, b_j \, Z_{ji}$$

In the present study, the method of extracting factors is the Principal Component method which basically uses the variable correlation matrix to yield the following relationship.

$$R_{jxj} = A_{jxm} \, A'_{mxj}$$

where R is the correlation matrix and A is the matrix of factor loadings a_{jm}.

The criterion used for extraction of factors is to maximize variance explained by each factor, that is,

$$\text{maximize} \quad \Sigma_j \quad a^2_{jm}$$

In the terminology of matrix algebra, this becomes an eigenvalue problem which is one of finding the eigenvalues of the correlation matrix given by:

$$\Lambda_{mxm} = A'_{mxj} \quad A_{jxm}$$

where each diagonal element of Λ_{mxm} gives the eigenvalues in descending order. Each eigenvalue represents the contribution of that factor to the variance. In Principal Component Analysis, one can extract as many factors as there are variables but using Kaiser's rule (Harman, 1967, p. 198) one limits the number of factors to only those whose eigenvalue or contribution to variance is at least one.

After extraction of factors, a rotation of factors is performed to yield what is known as a simple structure, which essentially means better interpretability of the factors with respect to the variables which are loaded on each factor. A method is used for this rotation in the varimax method, which is orthogonal rotation that makes the factor's invariant. In its simplest formulation the varimax criterion is

$$\text{Maximize} \; \sigma^2_{jm} = \frac{1}{n} \; \Sigma^n_{i=1} \; (a^2_{jm} - \bar{a}^2_m) \quad \text{for all } m$$

The result of this criterion is that of minimizing the number of high loading variables for a given factor.

The discussion on Factor Analysis is based on Rummell (1970) and Harman (196?

APPENDIX 4
DISCRIMINANT ANALYSIS *

The discriminantion problem can be stated as follows:

Given a sample of members from each of k known populations and values on variables for each member in each sample, the researcher is required to set p a method which (a) discriminates between the populations, (b) assigns a new ember to the correct population and (c) establishes the relative magnitude or importance) of the variables in the overall discrimination process.

In linear discriminant analysis, one finds a linear combination of a set f prediction (independent variables) such that the ratio of the between-group um of squares to the within-group sum of squares is maximal. An important ssumption in linear discriminant analysis is equal variance-covariance matrix or all groups.

If there are p predictor variables, x_1, x_2 .... x_p the linear combination s given by:

$$Y = v_1 x_1 + v_2 x_2 .... v_p x_p$$

If we denote the sum of squares of Y for k the group by $SS_k(Y)$, and let the ransformation vector $\underline{V}' = [v_1, v_2, ... v_3]$, we have:

$$SS_w(Y) = SS_1(Y) + SS_2(Y) + ...+ SS_,(Y)$$

hich is the within-group sum of squares. If we represent $SS_,(Y) = \underline{V}' \underline{S}_k \underline{V}_1$, hrough algebraic manipulation this can be represented in a quadratic form:

$$SS_w(Y) = \underline{V}' \underline{W} \underline{V}$$

here

$$\underline{W} = \sum_{k=1} \underline{S}_k$$

---

*The discussion in this section is a summary from Tatsuoka (1971), Cooley nd Lohnes (1971) and SPSS (1975).

Similarly, one can derive*

$$SS_b(Y) + \underset{\sim}{V}' \underset{\sim}{B} \underset{\sim}{V}$$ which is between groups sum of

squares. Now, if we represent the ratio $\dfrac{\underset{\sim}{V}' \underset{\sim}{B} \underset{\sim}{V}}{V' W V} = \lambda$, λ becomes a criterion for

measuring the group differentiation along the dimension specified by the vector V. This is called <u>discriminant criterion</u>.

Once the criterion is determined, the next step is to determine a set of weights $[v_1 \; v_2 \; .... \; v_p]$ which maximizes the discriminant criterion. These weights are called discriminant weights.

Though eigenvalue formulation one can derive the values of λ and associated with each λ is an eigenvector. The maximum number of eigenvalues one can extract is equal to k-1 or p which ever is smaller. Usually there are fewer groups than variables.

Finally, one can obtain as many discriminant functions as there are eigenvalues. A discriminant function is nothing but a linear combination of the predictor variables where the discriminant function coefficients are the discriminant weights. Thus, we have the first discriminant function:

$$Y_1 = v_1 \, x_1 + \, v_{12} \, x_2 + \, ... + v_{1_p} \, x_p$$

which has the largest discriminant criterion λ_1, and a second discriminant function:

$$Y_2 = v_{21} \, x_1 + v_{22} x_2 + \, ... \, v_{2_p} \, x \, p$$

with a discriminant criterion λ_2 which is the largest achievable by any linear combination of the x's that is uncorrelated with Y_1. We can derive more discriminant functions within the maximum possible number which is the smaller of

---

*The derivation of $\underset{\sim}{V}' \underset{\sim}{B} \underset{\sim}{V}$ is a little involved and can be found in many textbooks.

-1 or p. Although, a discriminant function can be derived it does not mean that it is significant in a statistical sense. There are usually fewer significant discriminant functions than the number extracted. Once a discriminant function is not found significant, by definition succeeding discriminant functions are also not significant and one can ignore all the non-significant discriminant functions.

The stepwise discriminating procedure selects variables sequentially for the analysis and retains at each that combination of variables with best discriminating power. Variables are dropped when found least useful.

The variable is considered for selection only if its partial multivariate -ratio is larger than an specified value. Similarly, variables are tested for removal only on their partial multivariate F, which must be smaller than a given value for removal to occur.

Classification is the final step in the discrimination procedure. It is the process by which a new observation is assigned to one of the k groups. The proportion of correct classifications indicates the usefulness of a discriminant function. A classification function for each group is derived from the pooled-within-groups covariance matrix and the centroids for the discriminating variables. The resulting classification coefficients are to be multiplied by the raw variable values, summed together and added into a constant. Thus, we have:

$$C_k = c_{k_1} x_1 + c_{k_2} x_2 + \ldots c_{kp} x_p + c_{ko}$$

where C_k is the classification score for group k, c_{kj}'s are classification coefficients, c_{ko} is the constant and the x's are raw scores on discriminating variables. There are separate equation for each group, and each case will have four scores. A new observation will be classified into the group with highest score.

A STATISTICAL PORTRAIT OF WOMEN* IN THE U.S.

Marital and Family Status

The rate of divorce has doubled during 1950-1975, and is declining, while the rate of remarriages has become stable since 1969 after only slightly increasing from 1950. Families with female heads has increased from 10.5% of all families in 1960 to 13% in 1975. The median age at first marriage has increased from 20.3 in 1950, 20.8 in 1970 to 21.1 in 1975. Among women 14 years and over 19.6% remained single in 1950 as compared to 19.0 in 1960 and 22.8 in 1975.

Fertility

The fertility rate has dropped during 1960-1974. For example, women 20 to 24 years old in 1960 had an average of 1 child each, but in 1974 the average was 0.6. The average for women 25 to 29 was 2 and 1.4 for the respective period. Children born to unwed mothers increased from 4% in 1940, 11% in 1970, to 13% in 1973 and the trend is increasing.

Education

For every 100 men who had completed 4 years of college in 1950, there were 66 women who had done so. The corresponding ratio in 1975 was 77. However, female college students in 1974 were in traditional areas, such as education (73%), English or Journalism (59%), health (64%). In 1949-50 about one fourth of all bachelor's and higher degrees were awarded to women, but only 10% of all doctorates. By 1972 the figures were 41% and 16% respectively.

---

*This section is abstracted from the publication with same title issued by Bureau of Census, April 1976, Current Population Reports, Special Studied Series P-23, No. 58.

Between 1950 and 1974 the number of women workers nearly doubled while
he number of men in the labor force increased by only 25%. The ratio of women
er 100 men in the labor force increased from 41 in 1950 to 63 in 1974. Among
6 years and older, 34% of the women were employed in 1950 compared to 46%
n 1974. The figures for males during this period are 87% and 80% respec-
ively. In 1950 only one-fourth of the married women were in the work force
ut in 1975 the rate went up to 44%. The projected increases during 1974-1990
re roughly the same for both men and women, i.e. 20%.

ccupation and Industry

Although employment of women increased substantially during 1960 and 1970,
omen remained fairly concentrated in a few major occupation groups. These
re secretaries, stenographers, typists, health service workers, elementary
chool teachers.

Most women (39%) in 1970 were working in the service industries with a
arge concentration (28%) in professional and related services. There was
n increase in representation in wholesale and retail trade; finance insurance
nd real estate; and relatively smaller gains in other service industries.

As far as work experience is concerned, the number of women with work
xperience increased from 29 women per 100 in year round full time jobs in
950 to 47 per 100 men in 1974. However, the median number of years that
mployed women have worked (3 years) has shown no increase in 1963 and 1973.

ncome and Poverty Status

Differences between the income of women and men workers remain sub-
tantial. In 1974 the median income of women year-round full time workers

-183-

was 57% of the median for comparable men. In both 1970 and 1974, the median income of women college graduates aged 25 and over who worked year round full time was only about 60% of the comparable male median income. In fact, women college graduates had incomes that were, on the average, lower than men with only a high school education. However, as the level of education increased to 5 or more years of college, the difference in the "pay-off" for education narrowed considerably. In descending order of female to male ratio, the professions are science and engineering (0.72 - 0.88), transportation, communication and utilities (0.66), professional and related services (0.60) and personal services (0.49) where the largest number of women are employed.

The contribution of the wife's income to the total income of husband-wife families has increased from 20% in 1960 to 27% in 1974.

The number of families with female heads has grown substantially over the past 25 years but the income has not increased in a relative sense. In 1950 families with female heads had a median income which equalled about 50% of the median for male-headed families; in 1974 this had dropped to about 47%. Although the per cent of all families with female heads below the poverty level declined from about 42% in 1960 to about 33% in both 1970 and 1974, the actual number of families in poverty increased between 1970 and 1974. For families with male heads both the number and per cent declined from 1960 to 1974.

BIBLIOGRAPHY

1. Aaker, David A. and George S. Day, Consumerism: Search for the Consumer Interest, New York, The Free Press, 1974.

2. Acker, Joan, "Woman and Social Stratification: A Case for Intellectual Sexism," John Huber, ed., Changing Women in a Changing Society, Chicago, The University of Chicago Press, 1973.

3. Ackerman, Gary L., "Child-Care Leave For Fathers?," Ms., Sept. 1973, Vol. 2, No. 3, pp. 118-119.

4. Alpert, Mark I., "Personality and Determinants of Product Choice," Journal of Marketing Research, Vol. 9, February, 1972, pp. 89-92.

5. Altman, China, "Only Skin Deep......," Ms., July 1973, Vol. 2, No. 1, pp. 23-25.

6. Anderson, W. Thomas, Jr., "Identifying the Convenience-Oriented Consumer," Journal of Marketing Research, Vol. 8, May 1971, pp. 179-183.

7. _____ and William H. Cunningham, "The Socially Conscious Consumer," Journal of Marketing, Vol. 36, July 1972, pp. 23-31.

8. Andreasan, Alan R., "Leisure Mobility and Life Style Patterns," American Marketing Association Conference Proceedings, Chicago, Winter 1967, pp. 55-62.

9. Arnott, Catherine C., "Husbands' Attitudes and Wives' Commitment is Employment," Journal of Marriage and Family, Vol. 34, 1972, pp. 673-681.

10. Astin, Helen S., The Woman Doctorate in America, New York, Russell Sage Foundation, 1969.

11. Bachrack, Stanley D. and Harry M. Scoble, Mail Questionnaire Efficiency: Controlled Reduction of Nonresponse.

12. Bailey, Kenneth D., "Cluster Analysis," David R. Heise, ed., Sociological Methodology, San Francisco, Jossey-Bass Publishers, 1974.

13. Bailyn, Lotte, "Career and Family Orientations of Husbands and Wives in Relation to Marital Happiness," Human Relations, Vol. 23, No. 2, 1970, pp. 97-114.

14. Baker, E. F., Technology and Women's Work, New York, Columbia University Press, 1964.

15. Bardwick, Judith M., Psychology of Women: A Study of Bio-Cultural Conflicts, New York, Harper and Row, 1971

16. _____ and Elizabeth Douvan, "Ambivalence: The Socialization of Women," in Gornick, Vivian and Barbara K. Moran "Women in Sexist Society," New York, Basic Books, 1971, pp. 145-1459)

17. Barickowski, Robert S. and James P. Stevens, "A Monte Carlo Study of the Stability of Canonical Correlations, Canonical Weights, and Canonical Variate-Variable Correlations," Multivariate Behavioral Research, July 1975, pp. 353-364.

18. Barry, Herbert, M. K. Bacon and Irvin L. Child, "A Cross Cultural Survey of Some Sex Differences in Socialization," Journal of Abnormal and Social Psychology, Vol. 55, November 1957, pp. 327-332.

19. Bass, F.M., E. A. Pessemier and D. J. Tigert, "A Taxonomy of Magazine Readership Applied to Problems in Marketing Strategy and Media Selection," The Journal of Business. XLII, 3, July 1969, pp. 7337-363).

20. Bauer, E. J., "Response Bias in a Mail Survey," Public Opinion Quarterly, Vol. 11, 1947, pp. 594-600.

21. Belkaoui, Ahmed and Janice M. Belkaoui, "A Comparative Analysis of the Roles Portrayed by Women in Print Advertisements: 1958, 1970, 1972," Journal of Marketing Research, Vol. XIII, May 1976, p. 171.

22. Bell, Gerald D., "Self-Confidence and Persuasion in Car Buying," Journal of Marketing Research, Vol. 4, February 1967a, pp. 46-53.

23. _____, "The Automobile Buyer After the Purchase," Journal of Marketing, Vol. 31, July 1967b, pp. 6-12.

24. Bem, Sandra L. and Daryl J. Bem, "Sex-Seggregated Ads: Do They Discourage Job Applicants?" Daryl J. Bem, ed., Beliefs, Attitudes and Human Affairs, California, Brooks/Cole, 1970.

25. Benson, Purnell H., "How Many Scales and How Many Categories Shall We Use in Consumer Research? - A Comment," Journal of Marketing, Vol. 35, No. 4, October 1971, p. 59.

26. Benston, Margaret, "The Political Economy of Women's Liberation," Monthly Review, Vol. 21, No. 4, September 1969, pp. 13-15.

27. Berger, Bennett, et. al., "Child Rearing Practices of the Communal Family," A. S. Skolnick and J. H. Skolnick, eds., The Family in Transition, Boston, Little, Brown Company, 1971.

28. Bergman, Barbara B. and Irma Adelman, "The 1973 Report of the President's Council of Economic Advisors: The Economic Role of Women," American Economic Review, Vol. 63, September 1969, pp. 509-514.

29. Berkowitz, Leonard and Louise R. Daniels, "Affecting the Salience of Social Responsibility Norm," Journal of Abnormal and Social Psychology, Vol. 68, March 1964, pp. 274-281.

30. _____ and Kenneth G. Lutterman, "The Traditional Socially Responsible Personality," Public Opinion Quarterly, Vol. 32, Summer 1968, pp. 169-185.

31. Bernard, Jessie, "The Status of Women in Modern Patterns of Culture, The Annals, No. 375, 1968, pp. 6-14.

32. _____, Academic Women, University Park, Pennsylvania University Press, 1964.

33. _____, "The Paradox of the Happy Housewife," Vivian Gornick and Barbara K. Moran, eds., Percent, Vol. 51, New York, Basic Books, 1971.

34. _____, Women and the Public Interest, Chicago, Aldine-Atherton, 1971.

35. Bieri, J., et. al., "Sex Differences in Perceptual Behavior," Journal of Personality, Vol. 26, No. 1, 1958, pp. 1-12.

36. Birnbaum, Z. W. and Monroe G. Sirken, "Bias Due to Non-Availability in Sampling Surveys," Journal of the American Statistical Association, Vol. 45, 1950, pp. 98-110.

37. Bishop, Doyle W., "Stability of the Factor Structure of Leisure Behavior: Analysis of Four Communities," Journal of Leisure Research, Vol. 4, Spring 1972, pp. 119-128.

38. Blair, William S., "Attitude Research and the Qualitative Value of Magazines" in Attitude Research at Lea, edited by Lee Adler and Irving Crispi, Chicago, American Marketing Association 1966, pp. 153-162.

39. Blake, Judith, "The Changing Status of Women in Developing Countries," Scientific American, Vol. 231, No. 3, September 1974, pp. 136-147.

40. Blalock, Hubert M., Jr., Social Statistics, 2nd edition, New York, McGraw Hill Book Co., 1972.

41. Blitz, Rudolph C., "Women in the Professions, 1870-1970," Monthly Labor Review, Vol. 97, No. 5, May 1974, pp. 34-39.

42. Blood, Robert O. and Donald M. Wolfe, Husbands and Wives: The Dynamics of Married Living, New York, The Free Press, 1960.

43. _____, "Long Range Causes and Consequences of the Employment of Married Women," Journal of Marriage and Family, Vol. 27, February 1965, pp. 43-47.

44. _____, The Family, New York, The Free Press, 1972.

45. Blumberg, Herbert L., Carolyn Fuller and A. Paul Hare, "Response Rates in Postal Surveys,", Public Opinion Quarterly, Vol. 38, Spring 1974, pp. 113-123.

46. Boh, Kotia and Stane Saksida, "An Attempt at a Typology of Time Use," Alexander Szalai, ed., The Use of Time, The Hague, Mouton, 1972.

47. Bonjean, C., D. McClemore, and R. Hill, Sociological Measurement, San Francisco, Chandler Publishing Company, 1967.

48. Boserup, Ester, Women's Role in Economic Development, New York, St. Martins Press, 1970.

49. Bryant, Barbara E., "Respondent Selection in a Time of Changing Household Composition", Journal of Marketing Research, Vol. 12, May 1975, pp. 129-135.

50. Bullough, Vern L., The Subordinate Sex, Urbana, University of Illinois Press, 1973.

51. Cadwell, Franchellie, "Shifting Female Market Will Kill Some Products," Advertising Age, Vol. 42, August 16, 1971.

52. Carden, Maren Lockwood, The New Feminist Movement, New York, Russell Sage Foundation, 1974.

53. Carpenter, Edwin H. "Personalizing Mail Surveys: A Replication and Reassessment," Public Opinion Quarterly, Vol. 38, Winter 1974-5, pp. 614 - 620.

54. Cattell, Raymond B., Factor Analysis: An Introduction and Manual for the Psychologist and Social Scientist, New York, Harper and Row, 1952.

55. _____, "Higher Order Factor Structures and Reticuler Versus Hierarchical Formulae for their Interpretation," Banks and Broadhurst, eds., Studies in Psychology, London, University of London Press, 1965.

56. Chafe, William H., The American Women: Her Changing Social Economic and Political Roles, 1920-1970, New York, Oxford University Press, 1972.

57. Clausen, J. A. and R. N. Ford, "Controlling Bias in Mail Questionnaires," Journal of the American Statistical Association, Vol. 42, 1947, pp. 497-511.

58. Clover, Vernon T., "Changes in Differences in Earnings and Occupational
     Status of Men and Women, 1947-1967," Department of Economics, College
     of Business Administration, Texas Tech University. 1970.

59. Cochran, William G., Sampling Techniques, 2nd edition, New York, John
     Wiley and Sons, Inc., 1953.

60. Cornfield, J., "The Determination of Sample Size," American Journal of
     Public Health, Vol. 41, pp. 654-661.

61. Courtney, Alice E. and Sarah W. Lockeretz, "A Woman's Place: An Analysis
     of the Roles Portrayed by Women in Magazine Advertisements," Journal
     of Marketing Research, Vol. 8, February, 1971, pp. 92-95.

62. Cox, Donald F. and Raymond A. Bauer, "Self-Confidence and Persuasibility
     in Women," Public Opinion Quarterly, Vol. 28, Fall 1965, pp. 453-466.

63. Crittenden, Ann, "Women Work and Men Change," The New York Times, January
     9, 1977, Business and Finance Section p. 22.

64. Cronbach, Lee J., "Coefficient Alpha and the Internal Structure of Tests,"
     Psychometrics, Vol. 16, September 1951, pp. 297-330.

65. _____ and Goldine C. Gleser, "Assessing Similarity Between
     Profiles," The Psychological Bulletin, Vol. 50, No. 6, 1953, pp. 457-473.

66. Dahlstron, Edmund and Rita Ligestron, "The Family and Married Women at
     Work," in E. Dahstron, ed., The Changing Roles of Men and Women,
     New York, Bantam Books, 1971.

67. Darden, William R. and Fred D. Reynolds, "Backward Profiling of Male
     Innovators," Journal of Marketing Research, Vol. 11, February 1974,
     pp. 79-85.

68. Darling, Martha, "The Role of Women in the Economy," Paris, Organization
     For Economic and Co-operation and Development, 1975.

69. Darlington, R. B., S. L. Weinberg and J. J. Walberg, "Canonical Variate
     Analysis and Related Techniques," Review of Educational Research,
     Vol. 43, 1973, pp. 433-454.

70. Davids, Leo, "North American Marriage: 1990," The Futurist, October 1971,
     pp. 190-194

71. Davis, Harry L., "Decision Making Within the Household," Journal of
     Consumer Research, Vol. 2, No. 4, March 1976, pp. 241-260.

72. _____, "Dimensions of Marital Roles in Consumer Decision Making," Journal of Marketing Research, Vol. 7, May 1970, pp. 168-177.

73. _____, "Measurement of Husband-Wife Influence in Consumer Purchase Decision," Journal of Marketing Research, Vol. 8, August 1971, pp. 305-312.

74. Davis, Susan, "How to Start Your Own business," Ms., June 1973.

75. Day, Robert C. and Robert L. Hamblin, "Some Effects of Close and Primitive Styles of Supervision," The American Journal of Sociology, Vol. 69, March 1964, pp. 499-511.

76. de Beauvoir, Simone, The Second Sex (Le Decuxieme Sexe), Paris, Gallimard, 1949, Translated by H. M. Parshley, New York, Bantam Books, 1970.

77. de Grazia, Sebastian, Of Time, Work and Leisure, Garden City, Double City, 1964.

78. Demby, Emanuel, "Psychographics and from Whence it Came," William Wells, ed., Life Style and Psychographics, Chicago, American Marketing Association, 1974, pp. 9-30.

79. Deming, William Edwards, Sample Design in Business Research, New York, John Wiley & Sons, 1960.

80. Dempewolf, J. A., "Development and Validation of a Feminism Scale," Psychological Reports, Vol. 34, 1974, pp. 651-657.

81. Deutsch, Helene, "The Psychology of Women," Vol. 1 and II, New York, Grune & Stratton, Inc., 1944, 1945.

82. Dichter, Ernest, Typology, Motivational Publications, September 1958, Vol. 3, No. 3.

83. Dixon, Marlene, "Public Idealogy and the Class Composition of Women's Liberation 1966-1969," Berkley Journal of Sociology, Vol. 16, 1971-72, pp. 149-179.

84. Dohrenwend, B. S., "An Experimental Study of Payments to Respondents," Public Opinion Quarterly, Vol. 34, 1970, pp. 621-624.

85. Donald, Marjorie H., "Implications of Non Response for the Interpretation of Mail Questionnaire Data," Public Opinion Quarterly, Vol. 24, 1960, pp. 99-114.

86. Donnelly, James H., Jr., and John M. Ivancevich, "A Methodolody for Identifying Innovator Characteristics of New Brand Purchasers," Journal of Marketing Research, Vol. 11, August 1974, pp. 331-334.

87. Dorney, Lester R., "Observations on Psychographics," Charles King and Douglas Tigert, eds., Attitude Research Reaches New Heights, American Marketing Association, Chicago, 1971, pp. 200-201.

88. Douglas, Susan P., "Cross-National Comparisons and Consumer Stereotypes: A Case Study of Working and Non-Working Wives in the U. S. and France," Journal of Consumer Research, Vol. 3, No. 1, June 1976, pp. 12-20.

89. Dowdall, Jean A., "Structural and Attitudinal Factors Associated with Female Labor Force Participation," Social Science Quarterly, Vol. 55, No. 1, June 1974.

90. DuBrin, Andrew J., Women in Transition, Springfield, Ill., Charles C. Thomas, 1972.

91. Dumazedier, Joffre, Toward A Society of Leisure, New York, The Free Press, 1967.

92. Duran, Benjamin S. and Patrick L. O'Dell, "Cluster Analysis - A Survey," Lecture Notes in Economic and Mathematical Systems - 100, New York, Springer-Verlag, 1970.

93. Edgerton, H. A., S. H. Britt and R. D. Norman, "Objective Differences Among Various Types of Respondents to a Mailed Questionnaire," American Sociological Review, Vol. 12, 1947, pp 435-444.

94. Edwards, Allen L., Techniques of Attitude Scale Construction, New York, Appleton-Century-Crofts, Inc., 1957.

95. El-Badry, M. A., "A Sampling Procedure for Mailed Questionnaires", Journal of the American Statistical Association, Vol. 51, June 1956, pp. 209-227.

96. Engel, James, David T. Kollat, and Roger D. Blackwell, Consumer Behavior, 2nd ed., New York, Holt, Rinehart, and Winston, 1973.

97. Epstein, Cynthia Fuchs, "Womena and the Professions," New Generation, Fall, 1969.

98. _____, Women's Place: Options and Limits in Professional Careers, Berkeley, University of California Press, 1970.

99. Erskine, Hazel, "The Polls: Women's Role", Public Opinion Quarterly, Vol. 35, 1971-1972, Summer, pp. 275-290.

100. Farrell, Warren, The Liberated Man, New York, Bantam Books, 1974.

101. Fasteau, Brenda F., "Giving Women A Sporting Chance," Ms., July 1973, Vol. 2, No. 1, pp. 56-60.

102. Fava, Sylvai, "The Statatus of Women in Professional Sociology," American Sociological Review, Vol. 25, April 1960, pp. 271-76.

103. Ferber, Robert, "The Problem of Bias in Mail Surveys: A Solution," Public Opinion Quarterly, Vol. 12, 1949, pp. 669-676.

104. _____, "Husband-Wife Influence in Family Purchasing Behavior," Journal of Consumer Research, Vol. 1, June 1974, pp. 43-56.

105. Ferriss, Abbott, L., Indicators of Trends in the Status of American Women, New York, Russell Sage Foundation, 1971.

106. Festinger, Leon and Daniel Katz, Research Methods in the Behavioral Sciences, New York, The Dryden Press, 1953.

107. Firestone, Shulamith, The Dialectic of Sex: The Case for Feminist Revolution, rev. ed., New York, Bantam Books, 1971.

108. Fisk, George, Leisure Spending Behavior, Philadelphia, University of Pennsylvania Press, 1963.

109. _____, Marketing and the Ecological Crisis, New York, Harper & Row, 1974.

110. Fogarty, M. Rhona N. Rapoport and Robert Rapoport, Career, Family and Sex Roles, London, Allen and Urwin, 1971.

111. Foote, Nelson N., Household Decision-Making, New York, New York University Press, 1961.

112. Ford, Robert N. and Hans Zeisel, "Bias in Mail Surveys," Public Opinion Quarterly, Vol. 12, 1949, pp. 495-501.

113. Fordham, Andrea S., "Ms. Conceptions by Women's Lib," The National Observer, July 12, 1975, pp. 18.

114. Frank, Ronald E. and Paul E. Green, "Numerical Taxonomy in Marketing Analysis," Journal of Marketing Research, Vol. 5, February 1968, pp. 83-98.

115. _____, and William F. Massy, and Donald G. Morrison, "Bias in Multiple Discriminant Analysis," Journal of Marketing Research, Vol. 2, August 1965, pp. 250-258.

116. _____, and Charles E. Strain, "A Segmentation Research Design Using Consumer Panel Data," Journal of Marketing Research, Vol. 9, November 1972, pp. 385-390.

117. Franzen, Raymond and Paul L. Lazarsfeld, "Mail Questionnaires as a Research Problem," Journal of Psychology, Vol. 20, October 1945, pp. 293-320.

118. Freeman, Jo, "The Tyranny of Structurelessness," Berkley Journal of Sociology, Vol. 17, 1972-1973, pp. 151-164.

119. Friedan, Betty, The Feminine Mystique, New York, Norton, 1963.

120. Frisbie, Bruce and Seymour Sudman, "The Use of Computers in Coding Free Responses," Public Opinion Quarterly, Vol. 32, Summer, 1968, pp. 216-232.

121. Fuller, Carol, "Weighting to Adjust for Nonresponse," Public Opinion Quarterly, Summer 1974, Vol. 38, pp. 239-246.

122. General Electric Company, Business Report, 1972.

123. Gianopulos, Artie and Howard E. Mitchell, "Marital Disagreement in Working Wife Marriages as a Function of Husband's Attitude Toward Wife's Employment," Marriage and Family Living, Vol. 19, No. 4, November 1957, pp. 373-378.

124. Ginzberg, Eli, Life Styles of Educated Women, New York, Columbia Press, 1966.

125. Gold, Sonia S., "Alternative National Goals and Women's Employment," Science 16, February 1973, pp. 656-660.

126. Gornick, Vivian and Barbara K. Moran (Ed.), Women in Sexist Society, New York, Basic Books, 1971.

127. Green, Paul E., Ronald E. Green, and Patrick J. Robinson, "Cluster Analysis in Test Market Selection," Management Science, Vol. 13, No. 8, April 1967, pp. B387-B400.

128. _____, and Vithala R. Rao, "Rating Scales and Information Recovery - How Many Scales and Response Categories to Use?" Journal of Marketing, Vol. 34, No. 3, July 1970.

129. _____, and Donald Tull, Research in Marketing, 3rd ed., Englewood Cliffs, New Jersey, Prentice-Hall, 1975.

130. Green, Robert T. and Isabella C. M. Cunningham, "Feminine Role Perceptions and Family Purchasing Decisions," Journal of Marketing Research, Vol. XII, August 1975, pp. 325-332.

131. Greeno, Daniel W., Montrose S. Sommers, and Jerome B. Kernan, "Personality and Implicit Behavior Patterns" Journal of Marketing Research, Vol. 10, February 1973, pp. 63-69.

132. Greer, Dean W., "The Application of Herbert Simon's Theory of Analyzing Social Movements to Women's Liberation," ERIC (ED 0758650) 1973.

133. Greer, Germain

134. Gross, Edward, "Plus Ça Change...? The Sexual Structure of Occupations Over Time," Social Problems, Vol. 16, No. 2, 1968, pp. 198-208.

135. Guilford, J. P. and Benjamin Fruchter, Fundamental Statistics in Psychology and Education, 5th ed., New York, McGraw-Hill Book Company, 1973.

136. Haavio-Mannila, Elina, "Sex Differentiation in Role Expectations and Performance," Journal of Marriage and Family, Vol. 29, No. 3, August 1967, pp. 568-578.

137. _____, "Sex Roles in Politics," Saffilios-Rothschild, ed., Toward a Sociology of Women, Massachusetts, Xerox Corporation, 1972.

138. Haley, Russell I., "Benefit Segmentation: A Decision-Oriented Research Tool," Journal of Marketing, Vol. 32, July 1968, pp. 30-35.

139. _____, "Beyond Benefit Segmentation," Journal of Advertising Research, Vol. 11, August 1971, pp. 3-8.

140. Hand, Horace B., "Working Mothers and Maladjusted Children," Journal of Education Sociology, Vol. 30, No. 5, 1957, pp. 245-246.

141. Haner, Charles F. and Norman C. Meier, "The Adaptability of Area Sampling to Public Opinion Measurement," Public Opinion Quarterly, Vol. 15, No. 2, 1951, pp. 335-352.

142. Hansen, Morris H. and Philip M. Hauser, "Area Sampling - Some Principles of Sampling Design," Public Opinion Quarterly, Vol. 9, No. 2, 1945, pp. 183-195.

143. _____, and William N. Hurwitz, "The Problem of Non-Response in Sample Surveys," Journal of the American Statistical Association, Vol. 41, December 1946, pp. 517-529.

144. _____, William N. Hurwitz, and William G. Madow, Sampling Survey Methods and Theory, Vols. I and II, New York, John Wiley and Sons, 1953.

145. Harman, Harry H., _Modern Factor Analysis_, 2nd ed., Chicago, University of Chicago Press, 1967.

146. Harris, Dorothy V. (ed.), _Women and Sport: A National Research Conference_, Penn State HPER Series No. 2, The Pennsylvania State University 1972.

147. Haug, Marie R., "Social Class Measurement and Women's Occupational Roles," _Social Forces_, Vo. 52, No. 1, September 19, 1973.

148. Havighurst, Robert J., "The Leisure Activities of the Middle-Aged," _American Journal of Sociology_, Vol. 63, No. 2, 1957-1958, pp. 152-162.

149. Hays, William L., _Statistics for the Social Sciences_, 2nd ed., New York, Holt, Rinehart, and Winston, 1973.

150. Heer, David M., "Dominance and the Working Wife," F. I. Nye and L. W. Hoffman, eds., _The Employed Mother in America_, Rand, McNally & Company, 1963.

151. Heerman, Emil F., "The Geometry of Factorial Indeterminacy," _Psychometrika_, Vol. 29, No. 4.

152. Heller, Harry E., "Defining Target Markets by Their Attitude Profiles," L. Adler and I. Crespi, eds., _Attitude Research on the Rocks_, Chicago, American Marketing Association, 1970.

153. Hemmerdinger, Elizabeth, "Demystifying Your Car," _Ms._, July 1972, Vol. 1, No. 1, pp. 36-38.

154. Hochschild, Arlie R., "A Review of Sex Role Research," _American Journal of Sociology_, Vol. 78, No. 4, 1973, pp. 1011-1029.

155. Hochstim, Joseph R. and Dilman M. K. Smith, "Area Sampling or Quota Control? Three Sampling Experiments," _Public Opinion Quarterly_, Vol. 12, No. 1, 1948, pp. 73-80.

156. Hoffman, Lois W., "Mother's Enjoyment of Work and Effects on the Child," _Child Development_, Vol. 32, 1961, pp. 187-197.

157. Holfer, Harriet, _Sex Roles and Social Change_, in Softilias-Rotheschild, 1972, pp. 333-343.

158. Holmstrom, Lynda L., _The Two-Career Family_, Cambridge, Mass., Schenkman Pub., 1972.

159. Horner, Matina, "Sex Differences in Achievement Motivation and Performance in Competitive and Non-Competitive Situations," Ph.D. dissertation, University of Michigan, summary report in _Psychology Today_, Vol. 3, No. 6 November 1969, pp. 36-38, 62.

160. Houseman, Earl E., "Statistical Treatment of the Non-Response Problem," _Agricultural Economic Research_, Vol. 5, 1953, pp. 12-18.

161. Howard, Nigel and Britt Harriss, A Hierarchical Grouping Routine, IBM 360/65 Fortran IV Program, University of Pennsylvania Computing Center, October 1966.

163. Jackson, J. A., ed., Role: Sociological Studies 4, London, Cambridge University Press, 1972.

164. Joesting, Joan, "Comparison of Women's Liberation Members with Their Non-Member Peers," Psychological Reports, Vol. 29, 1971, pp. 1291-1294.

165. Johnson, Frank A. and Colleen L. Johnson, "Role Strain in High Commitment Career Women," Journal of American Academy of Psychoanalysis, Vol. 4, No. 1, 1976, pp. 13-36.

166. Johnson, Richard M., How Can You Tell If Things Are Really Clustered?, Chicago Market Facts, Inc., 1972.

167. _____, Using Q Analysis in Marketing Research, Chicago, Market Facts, Inc., 1974.

168. Johnson, S. C., "Hierarchical Clustering Schemes," Psychometrika, Vol. 32, No. 3, pp. 241-254.

169. Kanuk, Leslie and Conrad Berenson, "Mail Surveys and Response Rates: A Literature Review," Journal of Marketing Research, Vol. XII, Nov. 1975, pp. 440-453.

170. Kaplan, Max, Leisure in American: A Social Inquiry, New York, John Wiley and Sons, 1960.

171. Kassarjian, Harold H., "Personality and Consumer Behavior: A Review," Journal of Marketing Research, Vol. 8, November 1971, pp. 409-418.

172. Katz, Elihu and Paul Lazarsfeld, Personal Influence, New York, Free Press, 1955.

173. Kelley, Robert F. and Michael B. Egan, "Husband and Wife Interaction in a Consumer Decision Process," R. L. King, ed., Marketing and the New Science of Planning, Chicago, American Marketing Association, 1969.

174. Keller, Suzanne, "The Future Role of Women," American Academy Political and Social Science Annals, Vol. 408, July 1973, pp. 1-12.

175. Kelly, John R., "Work and Leisure: A Simplified Paradigm," Journal of Leisure Research, Vol. 4, Winter 1972.

176. Kerlinger, Fred N., Foundations of Behavioral Research, 2nd ed., New York, Holt, Rinehart, and Winston, Inc., 1973.

177. King, Charles W. and John O. Summers, "Overlap of Opinion Leadership Across Product Categories," _Journal of Marketing Research_, Vol. 7, February, 1970, pp. 43-50.

178. _____ and Douglas J. Tigert, eds., _Attitude Research Reaches New Heights_, Chicago, American Marketing Association, 1971.

179. Kinner, Thomas C. and James R. Taylor, "The Effect of Ecological Concern on Brand Perceptions," _Journal of Marketing Research_, Vol. 10, May, 1973, pp. 191-197.

180. Kirkpatrick, Clifford, "The Construction of a Belief-Pattern Scale for Measuring Attitudes Toward Feminism," _Journal of Social Psychology_, Vol. 7, 1936, pp. 421-437.

181. Kish, Leslie, "A Procedure for Objective Respondent Selection Within the Household," _Journal of the American Statistical Association_, Vol. 44, Sept. 1949, pp. 380-387.

182. _____ and Irene Hess, "A Replacement Procedure for Reducing the Bias of Non-Response," _The American Statistician_, October 1959, pp. 17-19.

183. Knudsen, Dean, "The Declining Stratas of Women: Popular Myths and the Failure of Functionalist Thought," _Social Forces_, Vol. 48, December 1969, pp. 183-193.

184. Komarovsky, Mirra, "Cultural Contradictions and Sex Roles," _American Journal of Sociology_, Vol. 52, No. 3, November, 1946, pp. 184-189.

185. Komorita, Samuel S., "Attitude Content, Intensity and the Neutral Point on a Likert Scale," _Journal of Social Psychology_, Vol. 61, December, 1963, pp. 327-334.

186. _____ and W. K. Graham, "Number of Scale Points and the Reliability of Scales," _Educational and Psychological Measurement_, Vol. 4, November, 1965, pp. 987-995.

187. Kopenen, Arthur, "Personality Characteristics of Purchasers," _Journal of Advertising Research_, Vol. 1, No. 1, September, 1960.

188. Lagay, Bruce W.,"Assessing Bias: A Comparison of Two Methods," _Public Opinion Quarterly_, Vol. 33, Winter 1969-1970, pp. 615-618.

189. Lake, D., M. Miles, and R. Earle, _Measuring Human Behavior_, New York, David McKay, 1964.

190. Lazarsfeld, Paul, F., "The Art of Asking Why," National Marketing Review, Vol. 1, No. 1, Summer 1935, ppg. 26-38.

191. Lazer, William, "Life Style Concepts in Marketing," Toward Scientific Marketing, Proceedings of the American Marketing Association, December 1963, pp. 130-139.

192. Lehmann, Donald R. and James Hulbert, "Are Three Point Scales Always Good Enough?", Journal of Marketing Research, Vol. 9, November 1972, pp. 444-446.

193. Lessig, U. Parket and John O. Tollefson, "Market Segmentation through Numerical Taxonomy," Journal of Marketing Research, Vol. 8, November 1971, pp. 480-487.

194. Likert, Rensis, "The Dual Function of Statistics," Journal of the American Statistical Association, Vol. 55, March 1960, pp. 1-7.

195. Lipman-Blumen, Jean, "How Ideology Shapes Women's Lives," Scientific American, Vol. 22y, No. 1, 1972, pp. 34-42.

196. Long, Larry H., "Women's Labor Force Participation and the Residential Mobility of Families," Social Forces, Vol. 52, No. 3, March 1974, p. 342.

197. Lopata, Helena Z., Occupation Housewife, New York, Oxford University Press, 1971.

198. Mainardi, Pat, "The Politics of Housework," Robin Morgan, ed., Sisterhood is Powerful: An Anthology of Writings from the Women's Liberation Movement, New York, Random House Vintage Books, 1970, pp. 447-454.

199. Malabin, N. G. and Helen Young Waehrer, Women in a Man Made World, Chicago, Rand McNally and Company, 1972.

200. Mandell, Lewis, "When to Weight: Determining Non Response Bias in Survey Data," Public Opinion Quarterly, Summer 1974, pp. 247-252.

201. Marc, Marcel, "Using Reading Quality in Magazine Selection", Journal of Advertising Research, Vol. 6, December 1966, pp. 9-13.

202. Marcus, Alan S. and Raymond A. Bauer, "Yes: There are Generalized Opinion Leaders," Public Opinion Quarterly, Vol. 28, Winter 1964, pp. 628-32.

203. Martin, Thomas W., Keneth J. Berry and R. Brooke Jacobsen, "The Impact of Dual-Career Marriages on Female Professional Careers: An Empirical Test of a Parsonian Hypothesis," Journal of Marriage and the Family, November 1975, pp. 734-742.

204. Massy, William F., "Discriminant Analysis of Audience Characteristics," Journal of Advertising Research, Vol. 5, March 1965, pp. 39-48.

205. McCall, Suzanne, "Analytical Projections of Life Style Identification in Consumer Behavior," American Marketing Association Proceedings, 1976, pp. 354-359.

206. McClelland, David C., The Achieving Society, New York, The Free Press, 1967.

207. McKinney, John C., "Methodology, Procedures and Techniques in Sociology," Howard Becker and Alvin Boskoff, eds., Modern Sociological Theory, New York, The Dryden Press, Inc., 1957.

208. Mead, Margaret, Male and Female, New York, W. Morrow, 1950.

209. Meredity, William, "Canonical Correlations with Fallible Data," Psychometrika, Vol. 29, No. 1, March 1964, pp. 55-65.

210. Miles, Virginia, "The New Woman: Her Importance to Marketing," The International Advertiser, Vol. 12, No. 4, pp. 13-16.

211. Miller, George A., "The Magic Number Seven, Plus or Minus Two: Some Limits on Our Capacity for Processing Information," Psychological Review, Vol. 63, March 1956, pp. 81-97.

212. Miller, Judith and Leah Margulies, "The Media: New Images of Women in Contemporary Society," Mary Louise McBee and K. Blake, eds., The American Woman: Who Will She Be?, Beverly Hills, California, Glencoe Press, 1974.

213. Millet, Kate, Sexual Politics, New York, Doubleday, 1970.

214. Morrison, Donald G., "Measurement Problems in Cluster Analysis," Management Science, Vol. 13, No. 12, August 1967, pp. 775-781.

215. Moser, C. A., "Zuota Sampling," Journal of the Royal Statistical Society Series A., Vol. 115, pp. 411-423.

216. Mosteller, F. and P. J. McCarthy, "Estimating Population Proportions," Public Opinion Quarterly, Vol. 6, No. 3, 1942, pp. 452-458.

217. Mulligan, Linda W., "Wives, Women and Wife Role Behavior: An Alternative Cross-Cultural Perspective," International Journal of Comparative Sociology, Vol. 13, March 1972, pp. 36-47.

218. Myers, James H. and Arne F. Haug, "How a Preliminary Letter Affects Mail Survey Returns and Costs," Journal of Advertising Research, Vol. 9, September 1969, pp. 37-39.

-200-

219. _____ and Thomas S. Robertson, "Dimensions of Opinion Leadership," _Journal of Marketing Research_, Vol. 9, February 1972, pp. 41-46.

220. Myers, John G. and Francesco M. Nicosia, "Some Applications of Cluster Analysis to the Study of Consumer Typologies and Attitudinal-Behavior Change," Johan Arundt, ed., _Insights Into Consumer Behavior_, Boston, Allyn and Bacon, Inc., 1968.

221. Myrdal, Alva and Liola Klein, _Women's Two Roles - Home and Work_, London, Routledge, Kegan, Paul, 1960.

222. NARB, _Psychographics: A Study of Personality, Life Style, and Consumption Patterns_, New York, Newspaper Advertising Bureau, 1973.

223. NORC, _National Data Program for the Social Sciences_, Chicago, University of Chicago Press, 1974.

224. Nadler, Eugene B. and William R. Morrow, "Authoritarian Attitudes Toward Women and the Correlates," _The Journal of Social Psychology_, Vol. 49, 1959, pp. 113-123.

225. Neulinger, John and Miranda Breit, "Attitude Dimensions of Leisure," _Journal of Leisure Research_, Vol. 3, No. 2, Spring 1971.

226. Nichols, R. C. and M. A. Meyer, "Timing Postcard Follow-ups in Mail-Questionnaire Surveys," _Public Opinion Quarterly_, Vol. 30, 1966, pp. 306-307.

227. Nisbet, Robert, ed., _Social Change_, New York, Harper and Row, 1972.

228. Noe, Francis, "A Comparative Typology of Leisure in Non-Industrialized Society," _Journal of Leisure Research_, Vol. 2, No. 1, Winter 1970.

229. Nunnally, Jum C., _Psychometric Theory_, New York, McGraw-Hill, 1967.

230. O'Dell, William F., "Personal Interviews or Mail Panels," _Journal of Marketing_, Vol. 26, October 1962, pp. 34-39.

231. O'Neill, Harry, "Response Style Influence in Public Opinion Surveys," _Public Opinion Quarterly_, Spring 1967, Vol. 31, pp. 95-102.

232. Opinion Research Corporation, _America's Tastemakers: 1 and 2_, Princeton, New Jersey, Opinion Research Corporation, April and June, 1959.

233. Parsons, Robert J. and Thomas S. Medford, "The Effect of Advance Notice in Mail Surveys of Homogeneous Groups," _Public Opinion Quarterly_, Vol. 36, Summer 1972, pp. 258-259.

234. Parsons, Talcott, "The Social Structure of the Family," Ruth Nanda Anshen, ed., _The Family: Its Function and Destiny_, New York, Harper and Row, 1949.

235. Pearlin, Leonard L., "The Appeals of Anonymity in Questionnaire Response," _Public Opinion Quarterly_, Vol. 25, Winter 1961, pp. 640-647.

236. Pernica, Joseph, "The Second Generation of Market Segmentation Studies: An Audit of Buying Motivation," W.D. Wells, ed., _Life Style and Psychographics_, Chicago, American Marketing Association, 1974, pp. 277-313.

237. Perry, Michael and B. Curtis Hamm, "Canonical Analysis of Relations Between Socio-Economic Risk and Personal Influence in Purchase Decisions," _Journal of Marketing Research_, Vol. 6, August 1969, pp. 351-354.

238. Pessemier, Edgar A. and Albert Bruno, "An Empirical Investigation of the Reliability and Stability of Selected Activity and Attitude Measures," Working Paper No. 1632, Krannert Graduate School of Industrial Administration, Purdue University, May 1971.

239. _____, Philip C. Burger, and Douglas J. Tigert, Can New Product Buyers Be Identified?" _Journal of Marketing Research_, Vol. 4, November 1967, pp. 349-354.

240. _____, and Douglas J. Tigert, _Personality, Activity and Attitude Predictors of Consumer Behavior_, Proceedings, Summer 1966, Chicago, American Marketing Association.

241. Pogrebin, Letty Cottin, "Toys for Free Children," _Ms._, Vol. 2, No. 6, December 1973, ppg. 48-53.

242. Poloma, Margaret M. and T. Neal Garland, "The Married Professional Woman: A Study in the Tolerance of Domestication," _Journal of Marriage and the Family_, August 1971, pp. 522-531.

243. Rainwater, Lee, Richard P. Coleman, and Gerald Handel, _Workingman's Wife_, New York, MacFadden-Bartell Corporation, 1962.

244. Ramsey, Judith, "Those Vaginal Deodorants," _Ms._, November 1972, Vol. 1, No. 5, pp. 28-33.

245. Rapoport, Rhonda and Robert N. Rapoport, The Dual Career Family: A Variant Pattern and Social Change," Human Relations, January 1969, Vol. 22, No. 1, pp. 3-30.

246. Riley, Matilda W. and Anne Foner, "Leisure Roles," in Aging and Society, New York, Russell Sage Foundation, 1968, pp. 511-535.

247. Robertson, Thomas S., Innovative Behavior and Communication, New York, Holt, Rinehart and Winston, 1971.

248. _____, "Determinants of Innovative Behavior," American Marketing Association Proceedings, Reed Moyer, ed., 1967 Winter Conference.

249. _____ and James N. Kenneday, "Prediction of Consumer Innovation: Application of Multiple Discriminant Analysis," Journal of Marketing Research, Vol. 5, February 1968, pp. 64-69.

250. _____ and James H. Myers, "Personality Correlates of Opinion Leadership and Innovative Buying Behavior," Journal of Marketing Research, Vol. 6, May 1969, pp. 164-168.

251. Robinson, John P., Philip E. Converse and Alexander Szalai, "Everyday Life in Twelve Countries," Alexander Szalai, ed., The Use of Time, The Hague, Mouton and Co., 1972, pp. 113-144.

252. Rogers, Everett M. and David G. Gartano, "Methods of Measuring Opinion Leadership," Public Opinion Quarterly, Vol. 26, Fall 1962, pp. 435-441.

253. Rorer, L. G., "The Great Response Style Myth," Psychological Bulletin, Vol. 63, 1965, p. 149.

254. Rosenberg, Marie B. and Len V. Bergstrom, Woman and Society: A Critical Review of the Literature with a Selected Annotated Bibliography, New York, John Wiley and Sons, 1974.

255. Ross, Heather L. and Anita MacIntosh, "The Emergence of Households Headed by Women," Washington, D.C., The Urban Institute, Working Paper, 1073.

256. Rossi, Alice S., "Equality Between the Sexes: An Immodest Appeal," Deadalus, Vol. 93, 1964, pp. 6-7-652.

257. _____, "Women in Science: Why So Few," Science, Vol. 148, No. 3674, May 28, 1965, pp. 1196-1202.

258. _____, "Review of Ginzberg: Life Styles of Educated Women," American Scoiological Review, Vol. 31, December 1966, pp. 874-875.

259. _____, "The Status of Women in Sociology," American Sociologist, Vol. 5, No. 1, February 1970, pp. 1-12.

260. _____, "The Roots of Ambivalence in American Women,"
     Judith M. Bardwick, ed., Readings on the Psychology of Women,
     New York, Harper and Row, 1972.

261. Roy, Rustum and Della Roy, "Is Monogamy Outdated?' The Humanist,
     March/April, 1970.

262. Rulon, P. J., D. V. Tiedman, M. M. Tatsuoka, and R. R. Langmuir,
     Multivariate Statistics for Personnel Classification, New York,
     John Wiley and Sons, 1967.

263. Rummell, R. J., Applied Factor Analysis, Evanston, Northwestern
     University Press, 1970.

264. Safilios-Rothschild, Constantina, "Towards the Conceptualization and
     Measurement of Work Commitment," Human Relations, Vol. 24, No. 6,
     1971, pp. 489-493.

265. _____, Towards a Sociology of Women,
     Massachusetts, Xerox Corporation, 1972.

266. _____, Women and Social Policy, New Jersey,
     Prentice-Hall, 1974.

267. Scheuch, E., "Family Cohesion in Leisure Time," The Sociological Review,
     Vol. 8, No. 1, July, 1960.

268. Schmid, John and J. M. Leiman, "The Development of Hierarchical Factor
     Solutions," Psychometrika, Vol. 22, March, 1957.

269. Schoolman, Maria Joseph, "T-Shirts for Tea," Ms., February 1973,
     pp. 42-43.

270. Schultz, Theodore W., "Women's New Economic Commandments," Bulletin of
     the Atomic Scientists, February, 1972, p. 29.

271. Scott, Ann C., "Housework: For Love or Money," Ms., July 1972, Vol. 1,
     No. 1, pp. 56-59.

272. _____, "Closing the Muscle Gap," Ms., September 1974, Vol. 3,
     No. 3, pp. 49-55.

273. Scott, Christopher, "Research on Mail Surveys," Journal of the Royal
     Statistical Society, 1961, pp. 143-205.

274. Searls, Laura G., "Leisure Role Emphasis of College Graduate Home Makers,"
     Marriage and Family Living, Vol. 28, February 1966, pp. 77-82.

275. Sexton, Donald E. and Phyllis Haberman, "Women in Magazine Ads: 1959-71," Journal of Advertising Research, Vol. XV, October 1975, pp. 49-54.

276. Shaffer, Helen B., "Women's Consciousness Raising," in Editorial Research Reports on the Women's Movement, Washington, D. C., Congressional Quarterly, July, 1973.

277. Shaffer, Thomas E., "Psychological Considerations of the Female Participant," Women and Sport: A National Research Conference by Dorothy Harris, PennState HPER Series Number 2, The Pennsylvania State University, 1972.

278. Shaw, M. and J. Wright, Scales for the Measurement of Attitudes, Hightstown, New Jersey, McGraw-Hill Book Company.

279. Sheldon, Eleanor B., Family Economic Behavior: Problems and Prospects, Philadelphia, J. B. Lippincott Company, 1973.

280. Sheth, Jagdish N. and Douglas J. Tigert, "Factor Analysis in Marketing" paper presented at AMA Workshop on Multi-variate Methods in Marketing, January 21-23, 1970.

281. Shuchman, Abe and Michael Perry, "Self-Confidence and Persuasibility in Marketing: A Reappraisal," Journal of Marketing Research, Vol. 6, May 1969, pp. 146-154.

282. Shulman, Art, "A Comparison of Two Scales on Extremity Response Bias," Public Opinion Quarterly, Vol. 37, 1973 (Fall) pp. 407-412.

283. Smith, David E. and James L. Sternfield, "Natural Childbirth and Cooperative Child Rearing in Psychodelic Communes," Michael Gordon, ed., The Nuclear Family in Crisis, New York, Harper and Row, 1972, pp. 196-203.

284. Sokolowska, Magadelena, "Some Reflections on the Different Attitudes of Men and Women Toward Work," International Labor Review, Vol. 92, July-December, 1965, pp. 35-50.

285. Som, R. K., "On Sampling Design in Opinion and Marketing Research," Public Opinion Quarterly, Vol. 22, No. 4, 1958, pp. 564-566.

286. Spaulding, Denise, "Abortions: Legal But How Available?" Ms., Vol. 4, No. 3, September, 1975, p. 103.

287. SPSS (Second Edition) New York, McGraw-Hill Book Company, 1975.

288. Stafford, James E., "Influence of Preliminary Contact on Mail Returns," Journal of Marketing Research, Vol. 3, November 1977, pp. 410-411.

289. Steinem, Gloria, "Woman Voters Can't Be Trusted, Ms., Vol. 1, No. 1, July 1972.

290. Stewart, D. and W. Love, "A General Canonical Correlation Index," Psychological Bulletin, 1968, Vol. 70, pp. 160-163.

291. Stuteville, John R., "Sexually Polarized Products and Advertising Strategy," Journal of Retialing, Vol. 47, July 1971.

292. Sudman, Seymour, Applied Sampling, New York, Academic Press, 1976.

293. _____, Reducing the Cost of Survey, Chicago, Aldine Publishing Company, 1967.

294. Summers, Gene F., Attitude Measurement, Chicago, Rand McNally, 1970.

295. Summers, John O., "The Identity of Women's Clothing Fashion Opinion Leaders," Journal of Marketing Research, Vol. 7, May 1970, pp. 178-185.

296. _____, "Generalized Change Agents and Innovativeness," Journal of Marketing Research, Vol. 8, August 1971, pp. 313-316.

297. Sweet, James A., Women in the Labor Force, New York, Seminar Press, 1973.

298. Szalai, Alexander, (Ed.) The Use of Time, The Hague, Mouton, 1972.

299. Tatsuoka, Maurice M., Multivariate Analysis, New York, John Wiley and Sons, 1971.

300. _____ and David V. Tiedeman, "Discriminant Analysis," Review of Educational Research, December 1954, p.402.

301. Theodore, Athena, The Professional Woman, Cambridge, Mass., Schenkman, 1971.

302. Thorndike, Robert M. and David J. Weiss, "A Study of the Stability of Canonical Correlations and Canonical Components," Educational and Psychological Measurement, Vol. 33, 1973, pp. 123-134.

303. Tigert, Douglas J., "Can a Separate Market for French Canada Be Justified: Profiling English-French Markets Through LIfe Style Analysis," Donald N. Thompson and David S.R. Leighton, ed., Canadian Marketing Toronto, Wiley Publishers of Canada, 1973.

304. _____, "Life Style Analysis as a Basis for Media Selection," W. D. Wells, ed., Life Style and Psychographics, Chicago, American Marketing Association, 1974, pp. 171-201.

305. _____, "Psychographics: A Test-Retest Reliability Analysis," Proceedings, Fall 1969, Chicago, American Marketing Assotication, 1969, p.310.

306. _____, Richard Lathrope and Michael J. Bleeg, "The Fast Food Franchise: Psychographic and Demographic Segmentation Analysis," Journal of Retailing, 47, Spring 1971, pp. 81-90.

307. Trodahl, Verling and Ray E. Carter, Jr., "Random Selection of Respondents Within Households in Phone Surveys," Journal of Marketing Research, Vol. 1, May 1964, pp. 71-76.

308. Turner, Ralph, "Some Aspects of Women's Ambition," American Journal of Sociology, 1964, pp. 271-285.

309. U. S. Census Bureau. Census of Housing: 1970, Block Statistics, Syracuse, N. Y., Urbanized Area.

310. U. S. Department of Commerce, Bureau of the Census, Washington, D.C. A Statistical Portrait of Women in the United States, Special Studies Series P-23, No. 58, April 1976.

311. Van Gelder, Lindsy, "Coffee, Tea or Fly Me," Ms., Vol. 1, No. 7, January, 1973, p. 186.

312. Varga, Karoly, Marital Cohesion as Reflected in Time-budgets.

313. Venkatesan, M. and Jean Losco, "Women in Magazine Ads: 1959-71," Journal of Advertising Research, Vol. 15, October 1975, p. 51.

314. Villani, Kathryn E. A. and Donald R. Lehmann, "An Examination of the Stability of AIO Measures," American Marketing Association Fall Conference at Rochester, New York, August, 1975.

315. Wagner, Lowis C. and Janix B. Banos, "A Woman's Place: Follow-up Analysis of the Roles Portrayed by Women in Magazine Advertisements," Journal of Marketing Research, Vol. 10, May 1973, pp. 213-214.

316. Waisanen, F. B., "A Note on the Resposne to a Mailed Questionnaire," Public Opinion Quarterly, Vol. 18, Summer 1954, pp. 210-212.

317. Waldman, Elizabeth and Beverly J. McEaddy, "Where Women Work - An Analysis by Industry and Occupation," Monthly Labor Review, Vol. 97, No. 5, May 1974, pp. 3-13.

318. Ward, Joe H., Jr., "Hierarchical Grouping to Optimize an Objective Function," Journal of American Statistical Association, March 1973, pp. 236-243.

319. Weigand, Jonathan, "The Single Father," Ms., January 1973, Vol. 1, No. 7, pp. 29-32.

320. Weiss, F. B., "Female Earning Power May Equal Males as Early as 1985," Advertising Age, Vol. 42, December 20, 1971.

321. Wells, William D., "Backward Segmentation," Johan Arndt, ed. Insights into Consumer Behavior, Boston, Allyn and Bacon, Inc., 1968.

322. _____ , "Life Style Analysis and Psychographics: Definitions, Uses and Problems," William D. Wells, ed., Life Style and Psychographics, Chicago, American Marketing Association, 1967, Ch. 13.

323. _____ , "Psychographics: A Critical Review," Journal of Marketing Research, Vol. 12, May 1975, pp. 196-213.

324. _____ , "Segmentation By Attitude Types," Proceedings, Fall 1968, Chicago, American Marketing Association, 1969, pp. 124-126.

325. _____ , "Seven Questions About Life Style and Psychographics," AMA Proceedings, Spring and Fall 1972, Combined Series, pp. 462-465.

326. _____ , Seymour Banks, and Douglas Tigett, "Order in the Data," Proceedings, Winter, 1967, Chicago, American Marketing Association, 1967, pp. 263-266.

327. _____ , and George Gubar, Life Cycle Concept in Marketing Research," Journal of Marketing Research, Vol. 3, November 1966, pp. 355-363.

328. _____ , and Douglas J. Tigert, "Activities, Interests and Opinions," Journal of Advertising Research, Vol. 2, No. 4, August 1971, p. 31.

329. Whitehurst, Robert W., "Changing Ground Rules and Emergent Life-Styles," Roger W. Libby and Robert N. Whitehurst, eds., Renovating Marriage, Danville, California, Concensus Publishers, Inc., 1973.

330. Whyte, William H., Jr., "The Corporation and the Wife," <u>Fortune</u>, Vol. 44, 109 ff., November 1951.

331. _____, "The Wives of Management," Sigmund Noson and William H. Form, eds., <u>Man, Work, and Society</u>, New York, Basic Books, Inc., 1962, pp. 548-555.

332. Wilensky, Harold, "Women's Work: Economic Growth, Ideology and Structure," Institute of Industrial Relations, Reprint Series, No. 7, Berkeley, Calif., University of California, 1968.

333. Wilks, S. S., "Representative Sampling and Poll Reliability," <u>Public Opinion Quarterly</u>, Vol. 4, No. 2, 1940, pp. 261-269.

334. Willett, Roslyn, "Do Not Stereotype Women - An Appeal to Advertisers," <u>Journal of Home Economics</u>, Vol. 63, October 1971, pp. 549-551.

335. Wilson, Clark L., Marketplace Behavior - A Psychometric Approach, <u>American Marketing Association Proceedings</u>, Chicago, American Marketing Association, June 1966.

336. Wind, Yoram and Paul E. Green, "Some Conceptual Measurement and Analytical Problems in Life Style Research, Working Paper, August, 1972, The Wharton School, University of Pennsylvania.

337. _____and Arun K. Jain, "Higher Order Factor Analysis in the Classification of Psychographic Variables," <u>Journal of the Market Research Society</u>, Vol. 15, October 1973, pp. 224-232.

338. Wiseman, Frederick, "Methodological Bias in Public Opinion Surveys," Public' <u>Public Opinion Quarterly</u>, Vol. 36, Spring 1972, pp. 105-8.

339. Wolgast, Elizabeth H., "Do Husbands and Wives Make Purchasing Decisions," <u>Journal of Marketing</u>, Vol. 23, October 1958, pp. 151-158.

340. Wortzel, Lawrence H. and John M. Frisbie, "Women's Role Portrayal Preference in Advertisements: An Empirical Study," <u>Journal of Marketing</u>, Vol. 38 October 1974, pp. 41-46.

341. Yorburg, Betty, <u>The Changing Family</u>, New York, Columbia University Press, 1973.

342. Young, Shirley, "Psychographics Research and Marketing Relevancy," Charles W. King and Douglas J. Tigert, eds., <u>Attitude Research Reaches New Heights</u>, Chicago, American Marketing Association, 1971.

43. Zaltman, Gerald and Philip C. Burger, Marketing Research, Hinsdale, Ill.,
     The Dryden Press, 1975.

44. _____, Philip Kotler and Ira Kaufman, Creating Social Change,
     Holt, Rinehart and Winston, New York, 1972.

45. Ziff, Ruth, "The Role of Psychographics in the Development of Advertising
     Strategy and Copy," William D. Wells, ed., Life Style and
     Psychographics, Chicago, American Marketing Association, 1974.

46. Zober, Martin, "Determinants of Husband-Wife Aging Roles," Stuart H.
     Britt, ed., Consumer Behavior and the Behavioral Science, New
     York, John Wiley, 1966.

47. Znaniecki, Florian W., Social Relations and Social Roles: An Unfinished
     Systematic Sociology, San Francisco, Chandler, 1965.

About the Author

Alladi Venkatesh does research in the area of household economic and consumption behavior. His interests encompass the changing roles of women and their significance to household structure and dynamics. Presently, he is working on a grant from the National Science Foundation to study the impact of home computers on housework and family life.

He received his doctorate from Syracuse University and is currently on the faculty at the University of California, Irvine.